THE WILDERNESS

WHERE MIRACLES ARE BORN

BRIAN & CANDICE SIMMONS

BroadStreet
P U B L I S H I N G

BroadStreet Publishing Group, LLC
Racine, Wisconsin, USA
BroadStreetPublishing.com

THE WILDERNESS: WHERE MIRACLES ARE BORN

Stock or custom editions of BroadStreet Publishing titles may be purchased in
bulk for educational, business, ministry, fundraising, or sales promotional use. For
information, please e-mail info@broadstreetpublishing.com.

Cover design by Chris Garborg, GarborgDesign.com
Interior design and typesetting by Katherine Lloyd, theDESKonline.com

Printed in the United States of America

16 17 18 19 20 5 4 3 2 1

Contents

Chapter 1

The Wilderness: Everyone Has One

When you see the word *miracles* paired with *wilderness* in the title of this book, you might think, *Are you kidding?* We all love the word *miracle*, but *wilderness*—not so much! We've all experienced difficult seasons at one time or another and have hoped for that instantaneous miracle to appear. Over and over you can hear the cry of our hearts through the psalmist, King David, as he says:

"How long, O Lord?"

"When will you answer my cry?"

"Why must I wait so long for your promise to be fulfilled?"

We can all identify with those words, for we've all had unresolved issues surface in our journey with Christ. So in spite of what others may tell you, the Christian journey is not a life of endless bliss, with a perfect marriage, perfect relationships, and a perfect financial portfolio. Perfection can only be found in Christ, for the world we live in is a fallen world. And even though life is sweet for the lovers of God, we all still face times of unexpected trials, unpredicted difficulties, and seemingly unsolvable problems. In a word, this is the wilderness.

Every child of God will have a wilderness experience, but not everyone has to have a wilderness wandering. The "wilderness" is something every true Christ follower must pass through. The good news is you will make it through to the other side. However, let me tell you what many will not. You won't escape going through a wilderness or two on your way to paradise. The wilderness—everybody's got one.

There are at least ten named wildernesses in the Bible. Even Jesus entered into a wilderness season immediately after His baptism. He was tested with many ordeals. And the pathway to glory will invariably lead us through the wilderness. Between every promise and the Promised Land of fulfillment will be a wilderness. But the great promise of grace is always with us, for the Lord will never lead us into a path that He has not already ventured. He was victorious in His wilderness test, because He placed His hope in God alone and trusted in the living Word of God to sustain Him.

There's a children's song that my wife and I once taught our kids to sing as they were growing up. The lyrics are simple but the lesson they teach us is not.

My Lord knows the way through the wilderness,
All I have to do is follow.
My Lord knows the way through the wilderness,
All I have to do is follow.
Strength for today is mine all the way,

And all that I need for tomorrow.
My Lord knows the way through,
All I have to do is follow.

Follow, follow, I will follow Jesus.
Anywhere, everywhere, I will follow him.
Follow, follow, I will follow Jesus
Anywhere He leads me, I will follow Him.*

When you have no place to turn, and you feel like your progress is slow and your spiritual growth seems even slower, remember the words to that children's song, "My Lord Knows the Way." One step at a time and one day at a time, we move through our lives on this planet. Unexpected twists and turns come, but so does the glorious revelation that Jesus has gone before us through the darkest times of our lives and promises to take us through them to the other side, where all is glory and peace.

God's loving and watchful care over our lives is eternal. He has invested sacred blood and the life of His Son for us. He will never disappoint those who trust in Him. His ways are good and perfect. All I have to do is follow Him.

Open your heart to the truth we present in this book. Let it settle into your soul. You may want to read some of the chapters more than once to understand that your life is such a beautiful treasure to God that He will "polish" you with what seems like the abrasive sand of a desert-like experience.

In the pages that follow, we (Brian and Candice) share with you some of the difficult seasons we passed through while we were tribal missionaries in Central and South America. We

---

* Words and music by Sidney E. Cox, © 1951 Singspiration/ASCAP, all rights reserved. Used by permission of Brentwood-Benson Music Publishing, Inc. See: http://hymnal.calvarybaptistsv.org/291.html.

encountered demonic powers and were forced more than once to confess our deep need of Jesus. We will tell you stories of how God spared our daughter Joy after she was bitten by a large snake while playing at the river, and how we lost months of supplies in a flooding river. You'll read about our life journey as it unfolded over the years of our missionary career.

But the true story in this book takes place in the many wilderness encounters that the people of Israel faced after leaving Egypt in the powerful miracle recorded in the book of Exodus. The Israelites' stories give us insights into understanding our own stories—challenges of faith, delayed answers to prayer, and miraculous interventions that displayed God's glory. At the end of each chapter we've also included "God's Whisper," which are words of encouragement and hope we believe God has for you.

We're so glad you've chosen to read about our journey of faith. Jesus is the true Hero of our story, and we are thrilled to be able to share part of it with you. We hope you enjoy it and can find comfort and strength in whatever situation you face today.

All praises belong to the God and Father of our Lord Jesus Christ. For he is the Father of tender mercy and the God of endless comfort. He always comes alongside us to comfort us in every suffering so that we can come alongside those who are in any painful trial. We can bring them this same comfort that God has poured out upon us. And just as we experience the abundance of Christ's own sufferings, even more of God's comfort will cascade upon us through our union with Christ.

If troubles weigh us down, that just means that we will receive even more comfort to pass on to you for your deliverance! For the comfort pouring into us empowers us to bring comfort to you. And with this comfort upholding you, you can endure *victoriously* the same suffering that we experience. Now our hope for you is unshakable, because we know that just as you share in our sufferings you will also share in God's comforting strength.

—2 Corinthians 1:3–7

✥

CHAPTER 2

THE WILDERNESS: WHERE MIRACLES ARE BORN

It was our very first visit to the jungle as we were preparing to move in among the Kuna people as tribal missionaries. The hour-and-a-half flight took us into some of the deepest parts of the Darien Gap, a dense tropical rainforest that covers large portions of Panama and Colombia. We were finally moving to the village after years of prayer and preparation. Our hearts were pounding as we stepped down out of the Cessna 185 "bush plane." We were now in our new home, the Paya-Kuna tribal village of Pucuro!

Would the people welcome us? Would they be friendly to our family? Would their hearts be open to our message of new life in Jesus Christ? The first words we heard from the Kuna people were not what we expected.

"KILL BRIAN! KILL BRIAN!"

First it started with one man, then an entire crowd gathered at the jungle airstrip. They were shouting something strange: "Kill Brian! Kill Brian!" My first thought was, *That's a weird welcome. I hope it's not too late to get back into the airplane!*

As they saw the look of fear on our faces, they began to laugh! Just then, one of the men in the village quickly stepped forward and said to me in Spanish, "We're calling you 'uncle.'"

That was my first language lesson that day. I learned that the words *Kill Brian* meant *Uncle Brian* in the Kuna language! They were celebrating our arrival with cries of "Uncle Brian! Uncle Brian is here!" And so our adventure began. What would these days hold for us and our three small children as we would live in this forgotten jungle village? What challenges were waiting for us, and what dangers would lurk in the days to come? It was like a scene from *Survivor*!

Our life in the jungle was filled with many self-emptying opportunities to surrender our lives of convenience. Everything was out of our comfort zone: the heat, the language, the food, the outhouse—everything! We lived as the people lived, ate what they ate, and lived among them. Our wilderness exposed our weaknesses. It always does; that's the nature of every wilderness experience.

Consider this: as a servant of Christ, you will one day enter a season of helplessness where you no longer call the shots and know what to do. It will seem as if you don't have what it takes to survive—finding yourself in a place and a season where only Christ will be your strength.

The One whose name is Living Water is within you. This wonderful Jesus brings you a life-giving stream, fulfilling every need no matter how difficult the many surprises of life can be.

He is within you as a well of water "springing up into everlasting life!" (John 4:14).

This "springing well" begins to flow inside until praise rises up out of you again. Before you know it, the springs are watering everything around you—and every dry place within you. You will see things differently, you will feel differently about the people around you, and you will see things you didn't even notice before. When Jesus shows up in the wilderness, it disappears. It becomes a garden.

> The Lord will always show you where to go and what to do, filling you with refreshment when you are dry and in a difficult place. He will continually restore strength to you. You will flourish like a well-watered garden, and be like an ever-flowing, trustworthy spring of blessing. (Isaiah 58:11)

We learn in our difficult season that even though we may be *in* a wilderness, our hearts don't have to be a barren wasteland. Our wilderness starts growing flowers when Jesus flows from within us. His presence satisfies the deep thirst that dries up the soul and places us in a weary land or a weary season. Whoever heard of roses blooming in a desert?

> Even the desert will bloom like a rose. Every dry and barren place will blossom abundantly, singing joyously of the new day! (Isaiah 35:1–2)

Your wilderness (your life with its surprises and setbacks) will blossom with a rose; and that rose is Christ! Jesus, the Rose, will be found in your desert days, bringing a new fragrance and a new song. What you thought was an impossible climate for overcoming will become the canvas for a rose.

13

Miracles are waiting to be found in your wilderness. Even in a wilderness, God can work in power. He doesn't need perfection to pull off a miracle. He's done it before with nothing but chaos all around. It was called creation! There is no shortage of power with God. He can make lame ones leap and broken ones sing.

Most of us have an attitude that translates the word *wilderness* into "something terrible." In fact, the Bible teaches that the wilderness is the place where miracles are born, the place where we hear God speak, and the place where He truly reveals Himself to us. We have found our greatest difficulties in life to be the incubator of miracles!

What about you? Are you finding yourself in a wilderness? A difficult place where pressures surround you? Have you found the only way out is to lean on your Beloved?

MEETING GOD IN THE WILDERNESS

For nearly eight years, we lived in an actual wilderness. It was the jungle region of Central America known as Darien Gap. It had no road; it was so abandoned and obscure that the only way to get there was to take a dangerous river trip in a dug-out canoe or a flight in a small airplane that was designed to land on a short, grassy airstrip. And we had very few conveniences. No electricity, no running water, no Internet, no iPhone or Facebook. Thankfully our years of missionary training prepared us for what we faced, or at least for some of it! With our three children, we served as tribal missionaries with New Tribes Mission, reaching the forgotten Paya-Kuna people with the good news of Christ's love. It was a wilderness in more ways than one!

We faced various trials and tribulations during our time in the jungle. It seemed like every demon came out of the jungle to fight against us, starting with demonic powers that came when one of our daughters was bitten by a deadly snake and miraculously survived. And early in our ministry, we were targeted by the enemy when our narrow dug-out canoe overturned in a flooding river. We lost all the supplies meant to sustain us for months, and we nearly lost our lives.

These situations were major wake-up calls for us. We realized we needed to readjust the focus on our spiritual lens. Yet in the midst of our wilderness, we met the God of the Bible. God answered our prayers, and as a result He converted dozens as we asked Him to speak to the hearts of the people. God displayed miracles, dreams, and powerful signs and wonders on our behalf. Our family can testify that even a wilderness can blossom like a rose when we allow God to be everything to us.

God will even lead *you* there, into your very own personal wilderness. That's right. Just like the Hebrews, between you and your Promised Land lies a wilderness of discovery and, at times, disappointment. Yet in the wilderness we find that the surprises of life yield the most beautiful fruit. The supernatural power of God is more often displayed in a wilderness than in a church service. God will use your wilderness to release the virtues of Christ growing within!

GOD'S WHISPER

I know about your hard times. I'm moved deeply by that which troubles you—in your home, at work, with your family, with your health. I have never yet failed to help you when you have turned to Me. I have seen your hunger for more, and I have prepared a place for you at My table. Satisfying grace will be your portion. Mercy that sustains you even when you stumble—that will be the gift I bring to you. Even in your hard times, you have chosen to never leave Me. So I say to you, My beloved, I will never leave you.

✧

CHAPTER 3

THE WILDERNESS: A PLACE OF MYSTERY

We are all taking a journey through the wilderness, heading toward the land God has promised us. So what exactly is the "wilderness"?

The best definition I (Candice) can give you is this: it's a place in life you'd rather not be in, a place of dissatisfaction where you know something better exists. It can be the difficult place you find yourself in today. It can be an unfulfilling career, a broken marriage, or the sting of loneliness that doesn't go away. It's the place where you're humbled and stripped bare—the place of not knowing and not understanding. God may lead you on a path where a shroud of mystery covers your way.

Let's face it, at times we all walk into a place we didn't ask for, a place where we might never have chosen to go. If you're feeling crowded, stressed, and locked into a place you'd rather run from—that is your wilderness! It can be called a "season of discontent." It is a time in your life when you feel stuck, unable to get out of it on your own. It can feel like you're in a waiting room and you're thinking, *How much longer can I handle this, Lord?*

TESTING BEFORE THE MISSION

That has been my experience more than once. After we finished Bible school and our missionary training, we were ready to go to the mission field. We were ready to give ourselves to reach a tribe of people that had never heard the gospel. We were excited and knew that God was calling us. But we soon learned that knowing God's will is not the same as knowing His timing.

When we were ready to move forward, our finances had totally dried up. Brian had to step away from ministry for a season and find employment to take care of the needs of our family of five. God opened a door for him to work at an aircraft factory, where he was given the title "utility worker," meaning he was the one who fueled the airplanes when they first came out of the factory ready for their test flight. During the testing of the aircraft, he kept it fueled and ready to fly. But our hearts were set and ready to go to the mission field. We wanted to go to the jungle; fueling airplanes was never on our radar.

But it wasn't just the airplanes being taken on a "test flight"; Brian was also being tested. That season seemed to last longer than his patience. He still remembers the day he was fueling up a turboprop with his hands freezing cold, telling God that he loved Him more than ministry and that he would do anything just to be closer to Him. He would even fuel airplanes if that's what God wanted.

It wasn't very long after that prayer that the season changed. Finances came in, and we moved forward and set a date to go to Panama. God broke through the limitation of Brian's wilderness when Brian set God first in everything, including ministry. God is so good!

What about you? Have you been waiting and waiting for your season to change? Do you feel limited and confined in a place that can only be described by the word *wilderness*?

Some of the negative things associated with the wilderness include testing, trial, persecution, suffering, spiritual dryness, and what the ancient writers describe as the "dark night of the ✳ soul." But the positive, life-giving discoveries far outweigh the pain and perplexity of it all. We must return to authentic humility, simplicity, renewed gratefulness for the smallest of pleasures, the kisses of God that bring restoration, and the cup of joy running over again, even in the "jungle" of life.

EMBRACING THE MYSTERY

As a result of the fall, the wilderness became a physical reality on earth. But even though the wilderness was released on the earth as part of the curse, God is a redemptive God and uses the wilderness not as a means to harm us, but as a part of our spiritual re-creation. Satan's plan to harm us backfires if we allow the wilderness to do its perfecting work in us. The apostle Paul reminded us in 1 Corinthians 10:11:

> All the tests they endured on their way through the wilderness are a symbolic picture; an example which
> ✗ provides us with a warning, so that we can learn through ✗ what they experienced. For we live in a time when the purpose of all the ages past is now completing its goal within us.

So, *all* that happened in the wildernesses of the Old Testament was meant to be object lessons for you and me. It's true that we can learn from what they experienced, but that doesn't mean you and I are exempt from our own wilderness experience.

We wrongly assume that we must understand everything today. But there are questions that you cannot google an answer for. There are things and places that Wikipedia doesn't even have a listing for! We hate not knowing what God is doing in our lives, yet it is rare that we perceive the "why" until we graduate to our next season. In our wilderness we press for the meaning of the mysteries of our lives and demand answers that may not exist—or at least we are not meant to know why until we carry more of Christ within.

Somehow, in our wilderness, we must be content to not understand everything, to not be offended with God's treatment of us, and to be willing to "faithfully embrace the mysteries of faith while keeping a clean conscience" (1 Timothy 3:9). At times, some of the greatest miracles we discover in the desert are the miracles that God releases *within* us. Christ conquers our soul when we run out of answers.

Every mystery becomes a miracle if we will wait. Most of what Jesus taught was not always understood immediately by those who knew Him best. Later they understood what they had received. There must grow inside our souls a willingness to hear what we do not understand and treasure it within, even if we can do nothing about it until the time comes for the mystery to end.

We all want the miracles of God, but are we faithful to embrace the wilderness that is required to upgrade our hearts and make us ready for miracle power? New "apostolic technology" is available. It is the working of miracles—but it may take a day or two in the desert to get us there. So don't lose heart! Even in a wilderness, God can work in power. Often it takes a wilderness to make us desperate and thirsty for a move of the Spirit. We can expect no shortage of miracles, for God is with us no matter where we are. So what's there to fear? Nothing at all!

Things you've never planned are waiting for you as you walk on this path through the wilderness. This is the place where miracles are found, the place where glory waits and hides. A cloud of fire, a burning bush, a tabernacle of God's presence, a miracle in the making is waiting for you there. It is a sure promise that every believer can experience: your wilderness will bloom with new life, and the beautiful Rose will appear. So let's learn more about our destiny and how to find this place of miracles, this place called the wilderness.

GOD'S WHISPER

I am a God who stands watch over you at all times. My eyes rest upon you, not just observing you, but protecting you, keeping you in My care. I provide untold favors for you, guarding you from the temptation that is too great for you—all because I love you! When I consider you, My heart is stirred to act on your behalf. There is no need for worry or anxiety, for My hand is upon you and I will lead you. I ask for a deeper kind of confidence that goes beyond the moment and endures for a lifetime. Trust Me, and you will never be disappointed.

✦

CHAPTER 4

THE WILDERNESS: WHERE FAITH GROWS

As new believers, we became fascinated with the Bible. After seasons of soaking our heart in the Word of God and prayer for hours a day, God would give us dreams of reaching a tribe of unreached people with the gospel of Christ. More than anything, we wanted to go where no one had gone before and pioneer a kingdom outpost for our Lord Jesus. Our heart's desire was to be missionaries of the Lamb and to be the first people to share Christ with those living in spiritual darkness.

Our personal belief is that everyone that comes to Christ has had someone praying for them. A mother, a friend, or an intercessor somewhere—someone has prayed you into the kingdom. We certainly had those who prayed for us, a group of intercessors. They were elderly women who had stormed heaven for the youth of our community to turn to God. We both also had intercessors praying for us personally. Candice's aunt Mildred prayed her into the kingdom. Brian had some former high school buddies who had all been praying for him to come to Christ. Their prayers were answered powerfully as Brian turned from darkness to Christ on a Sunday morning. Jesus gripped his heart powerfully and captured him.

Our whirlwind romance began at a Bible study group and led us to our wedding day. We were convinced we could serve our King better together than apart. Missions would be our passion, our pursuit. Jesus wanted all of us, and we said yes to Him and yes to each other.

After four years of training and one year as a pastoral intern, we set out as a family for the jungles of Central America. We did not have an angel appear to us, telling us to go to the jungle as missionaries. God simply put an ache in our hearts that would not go away—an ache to see tribal people that had never heard the good news of Jesus Christ have a chance to hear the wonderful message of salvation.

We will never regret the times we only had a "maybe" and stepped out, only to find a miracle. We have had many times where we stepped out with a "perhaps," but each time it resulted in a great victory. We were weak, young, inexperienced, and perhaps even a little cocky, but we believed that when we acted in line with God's heart, we could usher in God's will. Perhaps you can imagine how we felt as we took our newborn son and two daughters into the dense tropical rainforest for the first time to reach a tribe with the message of Christ!

We had never met the Paya-Kuna people before, but we had seen them in our dreams. We longed to be the ones to tell them that Jesus was the Savior and that His Word would be their hope and joy. What a surprise when we were taken into the meeting hut, a large communal meeting place, and were greeted with these words:

"You might as well go back now and leave! The missionaries that came before you told us they loved us only to leave us when it became difficult. We have seen others come and tell us they would learn our language and give us God's trail [Word]. But they have all left us. We know you will leave us too! You might as well take your family and go back home."

Our hearts sank low as we heard those words. We assumed the people would be thrilled that we were willing to move into the midst of their poverty, learn their language, and give them the life-changing Word of God. Instead, they were hard, calloused, and at times even violent as we started to assimilate to their culture. There was one man in particular who seemed to want Brian dead. Even his secret Kuna name was ominous: Kill Morro. They never called him Morro, meaning "turtle," without using *Kill* with it. More than once he made us feel that if we dropped our guard, Brian might end up dead in the rainforest!

Yet something (or Someone) rose up inside of us, and we determined right then that we would not go home or give up. We would stay there no matter what happened—they could bury us there, but we would not leave them or turn aside until they had the Scriptures in their own language! Holy stubbornness can keep us in our calling. So many times the Lord promises us that we will reap if we do not faint or give up. "Keep going, and you will bear much fruit," the Lord seemed to say to us.

With God's unchanging grace and a revelation of His love, we can endure any wilderness and be faithful in any desert. The God of mercy, who understands our weakness, can empower us not only to do a miracle but to *be a* miracle of steadfastness, if we will only let Him take over our hearts. That was the greatest miracle we witnessed in the jungle—God would not give up on us!

Godliness Is Not Geographical

Let us tell you another secret we learned while on our jungle journey. Even in a wilderness, God will meet you and satisfy your heart with His presence. We often think that when we find our perfect place in the will of God, life will flow like a river of milk and honey. This is a fantasy and not a fulfillment of faith. Jesus was a tender plant in a desert land (Isaiah 53:2). He was the opposite of His surroundings. In a hard and dry place, God can make you tender and overflowing with His life within.

We must come to the place in our life when we can promise God that we will never let our relationship with Him be determined by where we live. I'm quite impressed with a lesson that Jeremiah can teach us through his parable of the ripe and spoiled figs (Jeremiah 24). The two types of figs describe the two types of situations God's people find themselves in. It was those who were taken into captivity in Babylon who were the "good figs." Those who were left in the holy land of Israel were the "rotten figs." Babylon, though an evil place, produced the good figs, while Judea, the good place, produced only rotten figs. Oh, how this speaks to our hearts!

The best "geography" is within you. The best place to be is not the easy place, but the place where we yield to Christ. The worst place to be is the place where we choose comfort over Christ. Your heart can be right even though your surroundings may be evil. Are you a "good fig" in a "rotten" place?

Haven't you found strength growing within even in the weakest place in your life? God is ready to pour Himself into your need if you will turn to Him as one who is "poor in spirit." There is a strategy in these last days to leave us weak—weak in ourselves so we can be strong in the strength of another. The great exchange takes place when we deposit our weakness in front of

His cross and ask for His divine strength. The surprise of the ages is that God delights in making weak ones strong. Let all the weak ones join us in this journey.

LET THE WEAK SAY, "I AM STRONG"

The Bible makes an amazing connection between miracles and troubles. To really receive a miracle means you must first have an impossibility facing you. Miracles come out of messes. The bigness of your problem only means a greater miracle ahead. Yes, God's greatest faith lessons come out of calamities.

> God will deliver you from trouble over and over again—
> until you understand that no matter what you go through,
> he will rescue you, and make sure that no evil will touch
> you! (Job 5:19)

Notice this verse teaches us that God doesn't always steer us away from trouble, but He majors in delivering us from our troubles. Trouble is a pretty good sign that God is with you! The three Hebrew children Shadrach, Meshach, and Abednego discovered that the king's order to heat the furnace seven times hotter was the perfect recipe for their miracle deliverance, and their fiery furnace was transformed into a four-man dance hall! Daniel found his greatest deliverance took place inside a lions' den. A greater Lion, Jesus, gave Daniel the courage that replaced his fear of lions!

Are you in any kind of trouble right now? If so, then you qualify for deliverance in the midst of your trouble as you set your love upon Him. If you compare your troubles to yourself, you are in trouble. But if you compare your troubles to God, your troubles are in trouble—they will have to bow before the King of all kings!

We are committed "Christian triumphalists." We believe that God triumphs over all. He triumphs over everything around us and everything within us. He triumphs over every spiritual foe and every spiritual flaw.

God's greatest goal for your life is not to just make life comfortable for you. He wants to build character. Listen to the words of a true apostle, the apostle Paul. Look at the lessons of his life and ministry. We can learn from him the redemptive value of all that comes into our lives. In 2 Corinthians 1:3–7, he encouraged us with these words:

> All praises belong to the God and Father of our Lord Jesus Christ! For he is the Father of tender mercy and the God of endless comfort. He always comes alongside of us to comfort us in every suffering so that we can come alongside of those who are in any painful trial. We can bring them this same comfort which God has poured out upon us. And just as we experience the abundance of Christ's own sufferings, even more of God's comfort will cascade upon us through our union with Christ. So if troubles weigh us down it just means that we will receive even more comfort to pass on to you for your deliverance! For the comfort pouring into us empowers us to bring comfort to you! And with this comfort upholding you, you can endure victoriously the same suffering that we experience. Now our hope for you is unshakable, because we know that just as you share in Christ's sufferings you will also share in God's comforting strength.

Can you see it? Your life is a blessing, and that blessing is released through the troubles you endure. God's love can make us happy no matter what we face. If God is going to make you like

Christ, then even enduring suffering for following Him will work a greater comfort and strength into your heart.

GOD TURNS SETBACKS INTO COMEBACKS

We are not a depressed couple, nor are we given to prolonged melancholy—yet we have gone through days we wished never happened! How about you? Have you ever been overwhelmed with a sense of, *Why do I have to go through this Lord? Do I have to take this test? Do I have to walk through this valley?* We have written this book, this personal story of ours, to hopefully give you some encouragement. Here's what we know to be true:

> So no matter what happens, we will not give up. For even if our outer person wears out, on the inside not a day goes by that we are not being renewed as we embrace a new kind of life! We view our slight distress and momentary troubles in the light of eternity. We see our difficulties as what unfolds within us an eternal, weighty glory far beyond any comparison. So we don't fix our gaze on what is seen, but on what is unseen. For what is seen [the wilderness] is temporary. But what is unseen [the glory] is eternal. (2 Corinthians 4:16–18)

This passage gives us the four reasons we don't get discouraged or lose heart:

1. We know our troubles are *slight*—the glory far outweighs any distress we may pass through. Even when your mind tells you different, begin to say, "The troubles around me are not as heavy as the glory within me!"

2. We know that all troubles are *temporary*—they don't last. Say to yourself, "This trouble won't last forever, but His love for me lasts longer than eternity!"

3. We keep our *eyes on God*, even when it's not easy. Say it from your heart today, "My eyes are fixed on the reality of Christ, not the troubles that are passing away!"

4. We know that God is using our troubles for a *greater eternal purpose*. It's time to say, "My glorious God has an eternal reward waiting for me. I know He will help me make it through this wilderness!"

These are the most important lessons of life. They are the anchors that keep us from drifting from God and what we know to be true. Yes, there are surprises ahead. Trusting God in the surprises of our lives makes us His true disciples.

Our journey will lead us down the path of the ancient Hebrew people as they were rescued from Egypt only to be taken through a process and a refining that required a wilderness. It's just the very process needed to transform us into the royal bride that will come up out of the wilderness leaning on her Beloved.

GOD'S WHISPER

More than riches, more than finances, you need My grace flowing through your life. I am the God of great provision. I have seen your needs before you ask, before you are even aware of them. My glory will take care of you, and My promise will never let you fail or be in want. I am the shepherding God who will lead you into the true riches that I have prepared for you. Even in your need, I am there to show you My love. Even as you consider what you lack, I consider how to bless you even more. Have you forgotten that My name is *Father*? And as your Father, I will care for you and provide for you. All that you need this moment I hold in My hands, so come to Me and find the overflowing love that is the inheritance of all who seek Me.

CHAPTER 5

✤

THE WILDERNESS: WHERE WORSHIP DEEPENS

The most difficult season of your life is about to be over. You will see a victory that will cause you to explode with joy and rejoice in song. The prophetic destiny of your life will be advanced, even in a wilderness of uncertainty. Miracles will be discovered in your wilderness.

We have found that miracles flow in an atmosphere of music. Worship turns a wilderness into an oasis of the supernatural. As we lived day after day in the jungle, it was the song of worship that kept us strong and submitted to our calling. The miracle of worship strengthened our souls. We would never want to live without worship. Heaven is full of the sounds of supernatural worship—musical miracles!

The Hebrews began their journey with an outdoor concert of praise on the banks of the Red Sea. They had just seen their enemy drown by a miracle of God's delivering power. That would make anyone sing!

Let's look at the miracle stories of Israel as they wandered through the wilderness. Their story is our story. Their miracles will be our miracles. We'll begin in the book of Exodus. This is where the miracles of Israel's wilderness began.

THE SONG OF MOSES

> Then Moses and the Israelites sang this song of praise to the Lord. (Exodus 15:1)

Did you know the wilderness miracles begin with a song? Worship always sets the stage for miracles. When the people worship, God comes out of hiding and shows His miracle power. It is amazing how worship triggers the supernatural release of heaven upon earth. As the people of God move from bondage into freedom, expect to hear singing along the way.

The journey through the wilderness actually began with the Song of Moses at the Red Sea. Before their very eyes, the waters of the sea honored the redeemed and moved aside to let them pass on dry ground. A million Hebrews witnessed this massive miracle! Praise began to stir within them. A celebration like you've never seen began spontaneously on the seashore as they watched their enemies float away.

The crossing of the Red Sea is to the Old Testament what the resurrection of Jesus Christ is to the New Testament. Both are astonishing examples of our salvation. The blood of the Passover lamb brought Israel out of bondage, but the parting of the Red Sea along with the Song of Moses delivered them from the power of Egypt.

Exodus 15 contains the first worship song recorded in Scripture. Many believe it is the oldest poem in the world. Moses is the author, and the glory of God is the theme. This is the overflow of a heart full of praise to Yahweh for His delivering mercies. Mourning had turned to dancing. Moses and the Hebrews were standing on resurrection ground, looking at the floating bodies of their enemies while rejoicing in the victory of God. Abandoned to the Lord, they sang together of His greatness.

The song of the saints forever will be the Song of Moses. You really need to study it, since this will actually be sung in eternity as we gather on the great sea of glass to praise almighty God. Music and worship will play an important role in our devotion to God in heaven. Redemption and glory will be the twin themes of our heavenly worship. Exodus 15 parallels Revelation 15. In both portions, we see God preparing a deliverer. In Exodus, it's Moses; in Revelation, it's a Man-child company of overcomers for the last days.

Exodus 15 and Revelation 15 are amazing chapters full of singing. As Moses and the redeemed stood on the shore of the Red Sea, with the light of a crimson dawn reflecting on its surface, it would have appeared as a sea of glass mingled with fire. The fire of the dawn had dyed its waters. Moses and the children of Israel were also a many-membered expression of Jesus Christ on the earth, shining with His fiery presence (see Isaiah 8:18 and Revelation 12:1–5).

It would be wise to learn this song of redemption and practice it for the heavenly choir—so you can join in with them!

Then I saw what looked like a vast sea of glass blended with fiery flames. And standing beside the sea were those who had conquered the beast, his image and the number of his name.* They each held in their hands the harps of

---

* All those who are one day victorious over the "beast" will learn to sing this eternal song of thanksgiving and praise. The "beast" is our self-life

God and they were singing the song of Moses the servant of God and the Lamb's song: "Mighty and marvelous are your miracles, Lord God, the Almighty! True and righteous are your ways, O Sovereign King of the ages! Who will not reverence you in awe, O Lord, and bring glory to your name? For you alone are holy and all nations will come and bow in worship before you, for your righteous works have been openly revealed." (Revelation 15:2–4)

It's true: one day our lives will become a song. The miracles in our wilderness will have finished the work in our hearts. The things that once troubled us will then be set to music and become the theme of our song. He will give you songs at the break of day!

The miracle of the Red Sea became a springboard for Moses to prophesy of what God would do for us in the days to come. The One who brought them out of Egypt will also bring us all into our inheritance. This prophetic song will become our future deliverance. It's the victory song for your wilderness!

GOD ON HIGH

"I will sing to the Lord, for he is raised up in the highest glory." (Exodus 15:1)

A life of miracles must be focused not on God's power but on His preeminence. The word *Lord* appears no less than twelve

---

(Psalm 73:22). It seems our beast life is quite active when we are walking in a wilderness season. But we are called to overcome this self through the life of Jesus within us. As we overcome by the power of the cross and borrow the life of Christ for ourselves, we qualify as overcomers who sing the sacred Song of Moses. All that is of the beast must be laid aside as we take up the Christ nature and live in His strength. He can change us from a beast to a lamb (Isaiah 11:6–10; Philippians 3:21; Revelation 12:11).

times in eighteen verses in the Song of Moses (Exodus 15:1–18); if you include all the pronouns for God, He is referred to thirty-three times in this song.

In our wilderness we tend to be so self-focused and consumed with our needs. But true worship is the worship of God, not just singing about our needs or our blessings. Worship is God focused, taking us out of our need into the glory fire of who He is and what He has done for us. Worship will release miracles in your life!

TRIUMPH OVER ENEMIES

"He has hurled the horse and the chariots into the sea." (Exodus 15:1)

Who else could have performed such a miracle as this? He has triumphed gloriously! Trapped between the devil and the deep Red Sea, the Hebrews cried out to the Lord, and the cloud of glory manifested as fire and light to them—yet to the horsemen of Egypt, it was total darkness. The beloved Hebrew people walked across in the supernatural light on dry ground. God has a way of dealing with your enemies. He drowned the horse and rider in the sea. He hurled them down to the mud and covered them with deep waters. No wonder the Israelites sang on the seashore! Your enemies will all one day be removed, and this great song of joy will be heard from your lips.

OUR STRENGTH

"Yah is my strength and my song of power!" (Exodus 15:2)

Yah is the name used here for God. *Yah* is more than simply an abbreviated form of Yahweh—it actually means the "God of

Power"! The power of God was unleashed at the Red Sea and is unleashed when we sing songs of power to glorify Him. The Hebrew word used here for *song* has often been translated as "power." The Passion Translation incorporates both concepts by rendering it, "Yah … is my song of power!" What is there to fear when this strong God is leading your life, even if the path takes you through a wilderness? What does it mean to have the Lord as your strength and song? Divine strength and the spiritual song are inseparable.

Jesus is about to become the song of the end-time church. We will finally enjoy Him as the very song our heart was meant to sing. We will sing this glorious song of the Lamb, and He will release strength to us as we do! As we sing, adoration will become transformation. Strength flows into us as worship flows out of us. We will be replenished, filled, and strengthened by the presence of God through worship. When the Lord becomes your strength, you will have something to sing about. He will actually become your song. The song of the last days will not be about us or what we have done—Jesus will be our very strength and song, no matter what comes!

Our Warrior God

"The Lord is a Warrior! Yahweh is his name!" (Exodus 15:3)

The Lord is a Man of War. One title of God is "the Lord of Armies." This is one aspect of the divine character that must be reemphasized in today's church: our Lord is a warrior. What you need in the wilderness is this Warrior who will fight for you. God will crush under His feet every foe to His purpose. Whether an army or an attitude, every foe will tremble at His name. How easily He won the battle for Israel! He simply hurled the armies of Egypt into the depths of the sea. Majestic power flows from this place of authority and shatters the enemies. That's worth singing about!

THE DANCE OF LOVE

It is His love and strength that takes us into God's heart, even in a wilderness. The two things the human heart craves are unfailing love and the power to change. These two basic needs drive nearly every activity of life under the sun. We are all looking for a love that will accept us the way we are, and we look for a strength that can transform us into who we yearn to become!

The Israelites not only sang at the Red Sea—they danced. They danced with all their might. Very soon you may find yourself dancing over the reality of your deliverance and victory just as Miriam danced. Miriam danced with a tambourine under a prophetic anointing, singing the chorus: "Sing to the Lord, for He has gloriously triumphed! The horses and chariots He has hurled into the sea" (v. 21). This prophetess was possibly ninety years old. Who said ninety is too old to dance? This Song of the Sea needs to be sung today. It's an easy song to dance to—ask Miriam. Your dancing days are still ahead!

GOD'S WHISPER

I have many levels of faith still waiting for you. Faith is like a river—it rises and at times it dries up. It is your weak faith that only looks at circumstances. I call you to assured faith that will believe My promises and brings Me glory. Your bold faith moves heaven and earth. I give to you this day more faith!

✤

CHAPTER 6

THE WILDERNESS: WHERE WE FEEL OUR LIMITATIONS

The truth of the wilderness is a strange truth to most of us. Why would God actually *lead* us into a wilderness? Our heavenly Leader will sometimes take us to a place where we are limited, walled in, and hindered from going forward. This is the first wilderness the Hebrews had to pass through, and so will we. It is the wilderness of Shur.

> Moses led Israel onward from the Red Sea into the Wilderness of Shur. For three days they trekked through the wilderness without finding water. (Exodus 15:22)

Shur is a Hebrew word that means "a wall, hemmed in, or limited." The name of this wilderness is significant. God led them along a wall. They could not escape this desert. Have you ever felt as if you have come to a place of restriction and limitation, making it impossible to move forward without a miracle? Have you ever felt like your back was up against a wall?

The Hebrews had followed the cloud to a wilderness of limitation. This was not because of rebellion or disobedience. It was because of God's perfect plan for their advance. Our loving Leader will always have a purpose in bringing you to the wilderness of Shur, the place of being walled in. This was the first test they were required to face in the desert!

Limitations are veiled opportunities to realize God's miracle provisions. There is a realm of plenty just beyond our limitations. We often come to the end of our hoarded resources only to find God's abundant supply is waiting for us. Miracles will happen in the land of your limitation. The end of your strength is the beginning of His!

God had proven Himself to them. There was no limit to His power, no end to what He would teach them. Notice the lessons everyone must learn as they move from spiritual captivity into freedom—a freedom that includes a wilderness! What is this place of barrenness that we all pass through on our way to our destiny?

Remember, *the wilderness is simply a place in life where you don't want to be.* Relationships that are not working, jobs you despise, and dreams that seem to never come true. All of these unexpected problems make up our wilderness. It is the place where the God of glory meets with the barren soul, showing us the deepest lessons of our lives. How we need the wilderness seasons to teach us more of God's ways.

WILDERNESS LESSONS

These are the five great lessons that must be learned from wilderness experiences:

1. *After you receive a new revelation, a test will follow.*

This often comes as a "pop quiz." Even Jesus faced this: "From the moment of his baptism, Jesus was overflowing with the Holy Spirit! He was taken by the Spirit from the Jordan into the lonely wilderness of Judea, to experience the ordeal of testing by the accuser for forty days" (Luke 4:1–2).

No sooner had Jesus heard the heavenly voice—"You are My beloved Son"—than he was led into a land of limitation where that word of Sonship had to be proven. God will bring tests before us to teach us His ways. It's not the devil but God who is guiding us to Marah's bitter waters. The cloud of glory will bring us to the water's edge. God will lead you into the wilderness just as He did His beloved Son. Your wilderness proves you are His beloved one!

The revelation at the Red Sea of God's ultimate triumph over every foe was followed by the trial and test of a wilderness where everything seemed to crumble around the Hebrews. The desert wilderness appeared as the very antithesis of the pristine garden of Eden. All its elements seemed in opposition to man. It was desolate, seemingly empty and barren of life. It was either too hot or too cold and a place devoid of hope. The desert in which the Israelites found themselves is described in Deuteronomy 8:15 as "a great and dreadful wilderness, with venomous snakes and scorpions, a dry and thirsty ground."

Perhaps the fact that the desert was the extreme opposite environment of Eden makes it the perfect place for us to meet with the Creator God. The barrenness reflects the effect of sin on the soul—a spiritual dryness and withering of fruitfulness and life. This realization should serve to draw us back to God's ways of wholeness and spiritual abundance. As basic supplies are scarce and self-preservation is of paramount concern, the desert is a place where God can exhibit His divine protection and daily provision of sustenance.

The starkness of the desert landscape mirrors the futility of human strivings and self-dependence; nonetheless, God meets us there and provides the vision and the means to reverse the curse Adam and Eve brought upon themselves in the garden. The wilderness is a test sent from God to reveal how much we trust Him in our discomfort. So remember: the next time God pours out His Spirit of revelation with fresh insight and wisdom and the glory begins to swirl around you, it is to prepare you for the lessons of the land of Shur. May our limitations release us to His fullness!

2. *Great problems often follow great victories.*

After a Red Sea, there's usually a desert! The Israelites were on their way to the Promised Land, but it was proving to be a difficult journey. What began with a dance of triumph became a desert of trial. We see Israel move quickly from the joy of victory to the bitterness of disappointment. Exodus 15:22 says, "Moses led Israel onward from the Red Sea into the Wilderness of Shur. For three days they trekked through the wilderness without finding water." Only three days into their journey, they encountered their first difficulty: a shortage of water. Expect some of your most difficult trials to come immediately on the heels of your victory! At times we assume that a continual experience of victory is the norm, when in fact, it is often sandwiched between the lessons we learn from our difficulties.

3. *Testing comes before resting.*

God has the right to bring into our lives whatever He chooses in order to make us more like Christ. When we turn our face to

Him in the midst of pain and impossibility, character and Christ-likeness are formed in us. Christians throughout the ages have discovered that God will turn everything into good if we will but love Christ through it all!

For three days the Hebrews found no water. Their reserve tank was running out. Thirst began to settle in. They were on the edge of death! What a disappointment following so closely on the heels of the glorious miracle at the Red Sea. They progressed from the parting of the waters only to arrive in a dry and barren land with nothing to satisfy their thirst. The seasons of our own lives are no different. We witness a miracle only to be "set up" for the test ahead. Miracles are meant to do more than fascinate our soul; they are meant to convince us that God's faithfulness will not fail when the dry desert days come. They knew Yahweh was powerful, but they did not know yet if He was good.

The glory cloud over their heads had led them through those three thirsty days, and that cloud was a constant witness that God was with them. The same pillar of cloud that saved them from Pharaoh was now leading them into a desert. God may lead *you* into the wilderness just as He did the Israelites and His beloved Son. The end result will be resting in the goodness of the One we love.

(4) *God designs our tests to teach us His ways.*

It is not the devil but God who is guiding us to the test of Marah's bitter waters. Exodus 15:23 explains, "When they came to Marah, they found water, but it was undrinkable and extremely bitter." The word *Marah* means "bitter, grief, or calamity." Israel came to this very place while walking under the cloud and in the will of God. They were not being punished. They were not being tested so that they would fail but that they would learn.

It was a three-day journey into the wilderness of Shur—three days without water! Three days is a picture of the resurrection realm. Under the cloud, led by God, they were walking in "resurrection life." The distance from the Red Sea to Marah was thirty-three miles. Jesus was raised to new life after being crucified at age thirty-three.

Sighting the waters after a three-day desert trek must have brought rejoicing to the Hebrews. Can you imagine how excited they were when they saw the glimmer of the surface of Marah's waters? Their thirst would be quenched, their livestock watered, and their reserves replenished. What a disappointment it must have been to discover that the waters were bitter and undrinkable! Their lives in Egypt were described as "bitter" (Exodus 1:12–14). Must they now drink bitter water? Now even their freedom became bitter at Marah.

God made the waters of the Nile undrinkable as a plague to hit the land of Egypt in order to free the Hebrews from their bondage. There is a relationship between the plagues of Egypt and the sweetening of the waters of Marah. The Egyptians were unable to drink the waters of the Nile because they failed to heed the command, "Let my people go!" (Exodus 7:16–18). Now God expected the Israelites to let the ways of Egypt with its compromise go from their lifestyle! They had left Egypt, but the ways of Egypt were still in their hearts. It was time to let "Egypt" go from God's people!

Their joy at discovering water was quickly turned to anger at Moses for leading them to such a place. How could Moses, the prophetic singer, bungle this so badly? Singing at the seashore three days before gave way to complaining at Marah. They spoke as if it had to do with Moses only. But what about that cloud of glory over their heads?

So the people vented their anger and grumbled against Moses, saying, "What are we to drink?" (Exodus 15:24)

We are no different in our reasoning. Oftentimes we put expectations on our leader to do something about circumstances and situations instead of God. We can witness a breathtaking miracle, like Moses leading the people through the Red Sea, and only three days later when a problem arises, we're convinced that it is God's leader who has led us wrongly. He or she must be the reason for the unpleasant circumstance!

Also, just like the children of Israel, we have often complained about our bitter situations. Amazing! We can sing and dance under the anointing one day and be grumbling the next. We gather on Sundays to worship and praise the One who delivered us from our sins, and then we fail to trust Him in the smaller details of our lives throughout the week. The same God that can handle the Red Sea can handle the bitter waters of Marah. So let's quarantine the virus of complaining and trust God to make our bitter waters sweet.

Often, when we are tested in life, we fail to see the problem as a spiritual test. We are quick to blame our Moses instead of looking to God, who is our guide. The Hebrews cried out to Moses for water but not to God. All of this took place while the pillar of cloud was over their heads. If they were led wrongly, wouldn't it have been God who made the blunder? Wouldn't it have been the leading of His cloud of glory that made the mistake and not Moses?

5. *We shorten the wilderness by seeing God's purpose in it.*

Have you ever felt like you were groping along a wall in the dark? Every one of us must go through the confining process of being led to places we would, personally, not choose. Like sheep led through a chute, the Israelites groped along in the wilderness until they were brought to Marah's bitter waters.

The sooner we learn the lesson of Shur, the sooner we are promoted and given grace to move out of that wilderness. But it must be heart-deep. Like the children of Israel, we have often complained about our bitter situations. We complain, "God, where is my miracle? Why can't I have another miracle like the Red Sea? Why won't You do something?" Just wait, dear one. The beginning of your miracle is even now at work *inside* you!

GOD'S WHISPER

Lean into Me. Lean into My Word and find all that you need. The rest I bring is sweet to your soul. It's time for Me to reshape your life. Let Me arrange the priorities and remove distractions. Your true life is discovered when you lean into Me. Weakness disappears and worries vanish when you lean into Me.

Chapter 7

✤

THE WILDERNESS: WHERE GOD PROVIDES A HEALING TREE

C an you imagine one day in the desert without water and having nothing for your children to drink? As one day became three days, the Israelites were passing out, falling over, and unable to go any farther. Their thirst consumed their every thought in every moment. Angry, bitter, and resentful—the people began to complain to the leader, "Why is this happening if God is with us? Why did God bring us into the desert to die of thirst?"

I (Brian) can remember one long day in the Darien jungle of Panama when I had nothing to drink. I had left the village to hunt wild pigs with the men without taking any water. We hadn't crossed any stream or rivers for hours, and I was thirsty! What a stupid thing to do! During the hunt, the young men of our village smelled the pigs and began to chase them. I ran and ran, but I couldn't get my gringo legs moving fast enough to catch up with the guys. Now I was lost in the jungle, like a scene right out of a movie. But it wasn't a comedy!

I would have to wait and hope the men would circle back around to see what had happened to me, or I could try to find my way back on my own. Maybe you can guess which one I chose. My male ego kicked in, and I didn't even stop to ask for directions. With no map or GPS, it wouldn't be easy, but I had an idea—if only I could find a stream, it would lead me back to the Pucuro River, where I could hopefully get my bearings. After hours of searching and praying for water, I'll never forget hearing the sound of the river. I was so thirsty—I'd never known a thirst like that before!

Jumping into the river, all I could do was drink and drink until the thirst vanished. And this was the result of only one day without water in the wilderness! What would it be like to go without water for three days in a desert?

Instead of striving with the critics of God's ways, Moses went before the Lord as a true servant of God and mediator. As an intercessor, Moses cried out to God for the people. God's miracle was found in a tree. Moses threw the tree into the water, and the water became sweet! Has the Lord shown you His tree, the one that makes your bitter waters sweet? Jesus is truly that flourishing tree spoken of in Psalm 1.

He is the "tree planted by God's design, deeply rooted by the brooks of bliss." A tree thrown into the water made the water sweet. What a clear picture this is of "the tree" upon which Jesus was crucified and how it can make the bitter things of our lives sweet. Jesus is the sweetener that is not artificial!

So Moses cried out to the Lord, and the Lord opened his eyes to see a tree. When Moses threw the branch of

the tree into the water, the water became good to drink.
(Exodus 15:25)

This we know: the cross has the power to turn sweet what
once brought bitterness to our lives. The sweetness of His cross
is stronger than the bitterness of abuse, pain, rejection, misun-
derstanding, or grief. The cross has yielded the most powerful
sweetness known on earth. By virtue of His sufferings, Jesus is
now dispensing power to take away our pain, turn our sorrow
to joy, and make our bitter experience sweet. There is honey for
us and healing for our pain. Throughout our "dark night of the
soul," we must hold to our hearts the cross of Christ like "a sachet
of myrrh" (Song of Songs 1:13). The sufferings of Christ actually
become a fragrant sweetness to a tender heart. If we will cry out
like Moses did, we will see the crucified Christ as our Healer.

GOD'S HONEY

There is another story in the Bible that shows how our difficulties
can become something sweet as we allow God to work in our
lives. It's the story of Samson, who fought a lion, but later found
hidden honey waiting for him. Samson was an amazing man—
the hippie judge who wanted a wife no matter what it might cost.
So he set off into enemy territory to find his wife, but along the
way he was confronted by a raging lion. Jesus also confronted a
roaring lion on the way to get His bride. Jesus faced the lion of
our sin, Satan himself. The cross was where Jesus was mauled
and pierced with the lion's claws (the nails). All for His bride, the
church.

So Samson, after killing a lion with his bare hands, went to
get his girl. Days later on his way home, he passed by the very
place where he had been mauled. He turned aside to look at the

lion's carcass, and what a surprise awaited him. "In the carcass of the lion was a swarm of bees and some honey. So he scooped out the honey with his hands" (Judges 14:8–9). Even what seems like devastation can yield honey. But who would want to wrestle a lion? Samson tasted sweetness out of what once brought him difficulty and struggle.

It's time for you to scoop the sweetness of Christ out of everything that troubles you. There is enough of God in every situation to give you honey if you will but turn aside and look. In Scripture, honey is often a symbol of the light of revelation. The deepest revelations and lessons of life come from the lions we meet along the way. Defeat the lion, and the honey is yours! It is like honey to our soul when we see the sweetness of God overwhelm the bitterness of our heart. That is, if we don't give up.

When we meet a difficulty or a test, it is not a sign of God's disapproval but an opportunity to taste God's victory in our lives. Look at the cross and you'll see it. Resurrection always follows refocus! Look at the pattern Jesus left us when He met the most difficult affliction of His life—to die on a cross. What a lion He faced at Calvary. But He suffered long enough, enduring the entire debacle so that His death would yield the honey of resurrection. Don't quit until *you* taste the honey!

Every desert trial we face has within it the seeds of a wonderful victory. If we lean on Him in our wilderness, those seeds will sprout and blossom, bearing the most pleasant fruit—all of this to our wonder and joy (Hebrews 12:2). Yet if we back off, throw in the towel, and give up, we are not giving God enough time to make the honey of victory.

Remember this: a wilderness is the place you *pass through* on the way to His heart. Listen to the courage of David when he faced a wilderness season in his life: "With you as my strength I can crush an enemy hoard, advancing through every stronghold that stands in front of me" (Psalm 18:29). Supernatural strength waits for you if you will turn to God in your most difficult moment. So often we're not prepared for the tests in life, but God is prepared to see us through them in victory.

Nothing had been said to the Israelites about commands and decrees while they were in Egypt, but in the desert they had to learn that blessings would flow to them as they were obedient to the covenant-keeping God:

> There the Lord made a decree and a binding promise on their behalf, and there he tested them. (Exodus 15:25)

The Lord tests us with every disappointment. He longs to prove Himself as the One who is more than enough. He lives in you and me and wants His endless life to come forth. You must "lay your hands on eternal life, for this is your calling" (1 Timothy 6:12). So we are called to possess a life that comes out of eternity, the life of our Lord Jesus.

Every test and trial is God's unique way of inviting us to lay hold of another life, a borrowed life, the life of Jesus. His life is enough for every pain and sorrow. It was enough on the cross to take away our burdens. He prevailed by laying hold of the life of His Father, even as He laid down His own life for us. But there is still more.

The Lord Who Heals

We may find ourselves walking in the wilderness, but it will take us into God's heart. I want to share with you the God who heals. He's a loving God who longs to bring you all the comfort and power you need to be healed inside and out. Let's take up the Hebrews' story where we left off. After the water was made sweet, God promised His people:

"If you listen carefully to the voice of the Lord your God and do what is pleasing in his eyes, if you follow his commands and keep all his decrees, I will not bring on you any of the sicknesses I brought on the Egyptians, for I am the Lord, your Healer." (Exodus 15:26)

Healing and listening to God's voice are linked together. The God who heals us is the God who wants us to pay attention to all His commands and follow His voice. We can trust what He says, for He is our Healer. We can do what He says, for He is our God. He can even heal your hearing problem so that you can hear His voice! He can heal your heart problem so you can follow His ways!

As we hear and obey, life is sweet. United to His heart, He makes the waters of Marah drinkable. Ask Paul and Silas. As they were in chains in a "Marah experience," they sang praises and glorified God. Bitter waters became sweet for them.

The One who healed the waters will heal you. Exodus 15:26 contains the first promise of healing in the Bible when God reveals Himself as Jehovah Rapha, saying, "For I am the Lord, your Healer."

The word used here for "heals" can also mean "to mend, to cure, to repair, to make healthy" and "to thoroughly make whole." One German scholar even translates it, "I am Yahweh, your Doctor."*

Here are some other powerful Scriptures that teach us of the "healing tree" of God's power. If you are in need today, here's your cure:

Yahweh, you are my soul's celebration.
How could I forget the miracles of kindness you've done
    for me?

---

* Hempel, *Theologische Literaturzeitung* 82 (1957): 809–826.

You've kissed my heart with your forgiveness,
    in spite of all I've done!
You've healed me inside and out from every disease!
(Psalm 103:2–3)

He heals the wounds of every shattered heart.
(Psalm147:3)

The Lord heals his fractured people and heals their severe
wounds. (Isaiah 30:26)

I love hearing this: "He heals all your sicknesses." Notice that
it doesn't say, "He diagnoses all your diseases." The doctor can
do that. Specialists can do a great job of putting their finger on
the disease and saying, "That's the cause." But they cannot heal.
Neither can any man. Only God can heal all our diseases: "I am
the Lord, your Healer!" (Exodus 15:26).

But it isn't just talking about diseases of the body, is it? Not
only can our bodies be healed but also our souls. He heals us
inside and out! The Hebrew word used in Exodus 15:26 for *sick-nesses* can also be translated "diseases, illnesses, grief, or wounds."
What a wonderful God who leads us through the wildernesses of
life! It was at Marah that this new revelation of God was imparted.
There's always a fresh and new revelation of God's healing power
in every wilderness. If we will but watch and listen, our cry for
mercy will be heard in heaven—and God will answer as our
Healer.

Look at Psalm 6:

No Lord! Don't condemn me.
Don't punish me in your fiery anger.
Please deal gently with me,
    show me mercy for I'm sick and frail.

I'm fading away with weakness.
Heal me, for I'm falling apart.
How long until you take away this pain
in my body and in my soul?
Lord, I'm trembling in fear!
Turn back death from my door and deliver my life
because I know you love and desire to have me
as your very own.
How can I be any good to you dead?
For those who are in the graveyards sing no songs.
In the darkness of death who remembers you?
How could I bring you praise if I'm buried in a tomb?
I'm so exhausted and worn out with my weeping.
I endure weary, sleepless nights filled with moaning,
soaking my pillow with my tears.
My eyes of faith won't focus anymore,
for sorrow fills my heart.
There are so many enemies who come against me!
Go away! Leave me, all you workers of wickedness!
For the Lord has turned to listen to my thunderous cry.
Yes! The Lord my Healer has heard all my pleading
and has taken hold of my prayers and answered them all.
Now it's my enemies who have been shamed!
Terror-stricken, they will turn back again,
knowing the bitterness of sudden disgrace!

If we seek God in our wilderness, we will find more than enough grace to move forward with confidence. We all visit Marah from time to time. As we take the healing tree and cast it into our circumstances, our hearts will be healed and our emotions balanced. Just as God used Marah in the maturing process of the Hebrews, so He will use our bitter experiences and heart-aches to lead us to His healing tree—the cross of Christ, the place of real healing.

So remember, the healing tree of grace can sweeten any difficult and calm any storm! Allow God to use what you have had to pass through to produce in you a strength you've never had before, a song you've never been able to sing before.

GOD'S WHISPER

I will bring you through seasons of silence, not for punishment but to perfect and mature your faith. The more glorious your calling, the more difficult your preparation. Ask My servant, Joseph. The silence of the pit and the chains of false imprisonment worked holiness into his soul. One day very soon, the designated darkness in your life will give way to the brilliance of a new day. Your prison doors will swing wide open to promote you as My godly champion to your destiny. Don't give up, falter, or complain, for your enthronement is near!

CHAPTER 8

✦

THE WILDERNESS: WHERE OUR ATTITUDES ARE ADJUSTED

What a journey we're on together. We have discovered that the Lord is our Healer as we "see the tree" that took away our sins. He was crucified for our full healing. Our bodies, our memories, and our emotions can be healed and made sweet by the revelation of the cross. If your thoughts are bitter, cast the cross into your attitude. If your body is broken and sick, cast the cross into your weakness. Healing comes as you see the abundant provisions of His cross. And the more you are healed, the more you will want to obey and follow His ways.

I (Candice) can remember harboring hatred and unforgiveness toward one of our closest neighbors in the jungle. She always seemed, in my opinion, to have a way of getting around every boundary I set up. She seemed to constantly take the first, the best, and the most of everything we gave out to the village; she seemed to always have a scheme and a plan; and she frequently sent her children over to our house and left them for me to watch. So my list of offenses went on and on. And to make things worse, I was feeling perfectly justified in those feelings. Until one day when my husband noticed that I had a slight tone that we can all get in our voices when we're condemning someone and enjoying it. And he confronted me. Oh no! I was busted!

The really bad thing is, I knew better. I was caught red-handed, which is not a good feeling. "Be sure your sin will find you out" (Numbers 32:23). How disgraceful of me to not love one of my closest neighbors. And so I went on a quest to have God change my heart. But even as I asked for forgiveness and tried my hardest to line up my heart with the Word, my condition was not lining up with my position before the Father. And it wasn't until one afternoon when our precious seven-year-old daughter was bitten by a five-foot-long Bushmaster snake that I was finally set free. God used an incredibly horrible situation to bring light and life to my heart!

HEALING THE ATTITUDES OF THE HEART

When I received the news that afternoon about the snakebite, my first thoughts were, *Lord are you chastising me? Have I done something wrong that I've brought this on our innocent little daughter?* And the Lord said, *No, your daughter will live, but while I have your full attention, I want you to know that you don't love my people.* As you can imagine, I was shocked! Immediately I thought to myself, *Okay, I don't love Mika, and now you're telling me that I don't love any of these people? Wow! I'm really a mess!* And as I watched our daughter struggle in and out of consciousness, I heard the Lord say, *You've entered into my suffering. As I watched my only Son dying upon the cross, I had to turn my back upon Him because of your sin. He carried your sin and I suffered for you! I sent my only Son to die for you. Can't you love these people for whom I've shed my blood? Were you any better than them when I brought you into my kingdom?*

Immediately it was as though the weight of unforgiveness lifted and love began to flow! His incredible outpouring of unconditional love was released in me. That did it for me! I was hooked on His love and forgiveness!

Forgiveness is the best investment you can make for your future and destiny. For as we have forgiven others, forgiveness and grace is heaped back on our plates. It's time to eat the humble pie of forgiveness. We've left a slice in the pan for you! There is something about forgiveness that takes us to the cross one more time to see the bleeding man taking our place and whispering forgiveness to the nail drivers.

Let go of the resentment instead of letting it grow. Ask the God who has forgiven you so much to give you His grace to forgive those who've hurt you. The feelings you harbor aren't hurting them at all, but they're killing you.

Above all, don't let Christians make you miss Jesus. Jesus never said, "Follow My followers," or "Follow My leaders." He said, "Follow Me." It's all about Jesus, the One who died for your sins so you wouldn't have to. It's ultimately Christ you accept or reject, not Christians. It's the cross you have to decide about, not the church. And it's Jesus you will meet when you've taken your last breath. All that's going to matter then—all that really matters now—is what have you done with Jesus? If you've never fully given yourself to Him as your only hope, don't let anything or anyone keep you from Him one more day!

Your wounds are not a reason to stay away from Jesus. In fact, they're a reason to run to Him. He's waiting, as He has been for a long time, with arms wide open to love you. Just throw the tree into your bitter waters and watch God make it sweet again!

And yes, for those who may be wondering, our daughter was healed and is alive and well to tell the wonderful story of her miracle today! Thank you, Lord!

Making the Right Choices

The time has come for God to adjust our hearts and open us up to more of who He really is. There is so much more of God to discover, but we have to make the choice to learn from the Master Potter, our Father God. Perhaps the hardest thing to do is where we need to start. What is the hardest thing to do when you're in a wilderness season? Rejoice. That's right, to rejoice is a choice we make even when our situations are not the best.

We all want our way. Our preferences would always be to have perfect surroundings with fluffy clouds of peace we could float on and over every painful event. But it is making the choice to rejoice that sets us apart as God's people. Rejoicing in the midst of difficulty is giving God what He wants: surrendered worship. When a heart refuses to focus on anything but God, we choose to honor Him with our praises. We have found in our less-than-trouble-free lives that when we leave our pain behind and turn our faces to heaven with joy and celebration, our hearts are changed, and eventually, our circumstance will also change. Pain will yield to the praises of abandoned lovers who pour out upon Jesus the sweet praises of our lives.

You can have the right attitude of joy throughout your life, and the secret is found in three words. Can you guess what they might be? Some are convinced the three words are: "retirement has come," or "finally got married," or "stocks are up." The three words that are the beginning of a life of joy are these: *Jesus is Lord*.

How do we make that work? The truth is, God will use our imperfect circumstances to accomplish His perfect plan for our life. A wilderness and joy have one thing in common—both must be worked out in our hearts. When we can praise our way through pain, we are on the pathway out of the wilderness. It is by leaning upon our Beloved that we come up out of the spiritual dryness of a desert-like experience. The Song of Songs 8:5 describes this process: "Who is this coming up from the desert leaning on her Lover?" The answer is, it is you. The desert has not defeated you and never will when you make the right choice and adopt a lifestyle of joy in the Lord.

GOD'S WHISPER

Ask Me, and you will receive. My name is Extravagant Giver! I will answer the cry of the tender ones who come before Me. Wisdom is waiting to open the door of guidance into your future. Knock on wisdom's door, and it will open to you! Seek me as a thirsty one seeks water, as a hungry one seeks food. For those who seek Me, the great revelation will come—I am easy to find! Keep coming and don't be fatigued in your praying to Me. The Holy Spirit will be given to you in even greater ways when you ask Me as your Father. My kingdom of beauty is waiting for you to ask, seek, and knock.

✤

CHAPTER 9

THE WILDERNESS: AN OASIS IN HIDING

Who said life has to always be difficult? God seems to sprinkle our problems with heavenly surprises of joy. There really is an oasis up ahead—a place with flowing streams and palm trees waiting for you on your journey if you'll just keep going!

We all too often measure our life by our weaknesses instead of His breakthroughs, by our difficult day instead of a glorious decade, or by the momentary mess instead of the amazing miracle of grace. Soon our measurements will change. We will be absorbed by the gaze of the fiery Lover who comes to consume us into the living flames. Then we'll measure our life by eternity's treasures and love's conquest.

In Exodus 5:1, God made it clear that the reason He wanted to take His people into the wilderness was so that they could feast with Him. He said, "Release My people, so that they may feast with Me in the wilderness!" That's right, a feast is waiting in your wilderness.

This verse is astounding, for it teaches us that what we call a barren desert, God calls a place to hold a feast. Do you feel like you are locked into a desolate place with difficulty surrounding you? Even there, a feast awaits. God has the power to turn the wilderness into an oasis.

God is never embarrassed to start over. He never fails, but He will take our failures, reverse them, and bring us into ultimate victory. Our life pathway may lead through dark valleys, but that is only so we can arrive at the oasis of bliss waiting ahead.

An Oasis Named Elim

So once again, God was starting over with His people, and He would accomplish His divine purpose through their experience in the wilderness. After their bitter experience at Marah and the amazing miracle of the tree, Israel moved on under the cloud to Elim. What a pleasant place compared to Marah! Only seven miles from Marah, twelve springs of water and seventy palm trees were waiting to refresh their hearts. Elim was a place of renewal and refreshing:

> Then they came to an oasis named Elim. It was a place of twelve springs and seventy palm trees. So at Elim they made their camp beside the springs. (Exodus 15:27)

What purpose could the Holy Spirit have for numbering the palm trees and the springs? Everything in the Scriptures has significance. The number seventy is very important. It was the number of Jacob's family that went down into Egypt. Seventy souls were moved from the Promised Land during a time of famine and settled in Goshen (Genesis 46). Seventy is the number that represents God's people carrying out His purposes. Jesus called twelve apostles to Himself and later sent out seventy disciples to preach the message of the kingdom. Twelve is the biblical number for the people of God: twelve tribes of Israel and twelve apostles of Jesus.

For every tribe there was a spring. For every disciple there was a palm at Elim. Seventy palms and twelve springs is a symbolic promise to you and I that we will carry out God's purpose. He will not lead us into a wilderness without leading us out refreshed and victorious! We will be stronger than the day we went in! These numbers, twelve and seventy, symbolically teach us that our covenant with God is still on—even in the desert.

Twelve is also the number of the months of the year. Seventy years is the minimum length of life the Lord has promised us in Psalm 90:10. At Elim's oasis, there was a spring for every month and a palm tree for every year. This tells us God wants us to be fruitful all the days of our lives, in our youth and in our old age. God has as many palms as He has years for you. The people under the cloud flourished like palm trees: "The righteous will flourish like a palm tree" (Psalm 92:12).

A place of rest and refreshment is to be yours each month and each year of your life! The God of covenant had led them to Elim as a sign that He would fulfill His promises and give them strength for the journey.

Under the Swaying Palms

Elim is a plural noun in Hebrew that means "the mighty ones," or "the strong ones." At Elim there were seventy tall, strong palm trees that represented victory and twelve refreshing pools to renew the Hebrews' strength. Elim was a picture of God's people walking in resurrection power. A Marah experience of bitterness will bring us to an Elim encounter of refreshment. Under the swaying palms, we become God's mighty ones, His strong ones who have borrowed their strength from Him.

The trees grew upward, and the springs flowed outward. Resurrection life flows upward, and the living presence of Christ flows outward from inside of us. Connected to His life and as we allow "the tree" to turn our bitterness into sweetness, miracles will manifest. Elim is God's garden, His plantation of pleasure. Both Eden and Elim are pictures of what God longs to bring forth in the heart of His people. Ultimately, God will make us His New Jerusalem bride. Human and divine mingle together at Elim and the New Jerusalem. The twelve springs are for the mingling of human and divine. They signify God's life flowing as a living spring into His chosen people and establishing them for His eternal purpose.

The twelve apostles were like twelve springs that watered the earth. God flowed from their lives into the people of the world. All who believe in Christ will likewise become "walking wells of life" to the nations of the earth. Christ in you is the supply of water and the source of refreshing while in your wilderness. The springs of Elim flow through you as the oasis of His love. Inside of you is a bubbling fountain, a well springing up with everlasting life. Your Friend in the desert says, "Whoever believes in Me, as the Scripture has said, streams of living water will flow from within him!" These streams of John 7:38 are the springs of Exodus 15. God's people, like the Hebrews at Elim, are bubbling with life as if they were springs of water.

Jesus is that never-failing stream when every other brook dries up. We are the desert that blossoms when Christ overflows!

The Lord will always show you where to go and what to do, filling you with refreshment when you are dry, and in a difficult place. He will continually restore strength to you. You will flourish like a well-watered garden, and be like an ever-flowing, trustworthy spring of blessing (Isaiah 58:11).

This oasis in the desert was only seven miles away from the bitter, undrinkable water! Could they not trust the Lord for another *seven* miles? That would be about a day's journey for those in the desert. Can you make it just one more day? Up ahead and around the bend is a pleasant pool of refreshing where the gushing springs make the palm trees flourish. Jesus is our fountain of living water (Jeremiah 2:13). He is worth the wait. He is worth the journey.

"They made their camp beside the springs" (Exodus 15:27). The camp of the Hebrews was a military encampment. They had been formed into an army. When God refreshes our hearts, it is so that we will be prepared for battle. An oasis becomes our school—the place of preparation for what lies ahead. Soon, they would wage war as an army, but for the moment they needed to be refreshed.

How wonderful it is when the churches of a region camp at Elim, near the water, where their sons turn into soldiers. Thirsting ones become triumphant ones. So here's the plan: What do you say we go and camp at Elim until we overflow? Sounds good to me!

GOD'S WHISPER

<u>New grace for a new day is being poured out upon you.</u> A new awakening to My purpose for your life and the provision for this day. Have you not asked Me for your family? Have you not asked me for your needs? I will never neglect My own; I will provide all that you have asked for. My name is Endless Love, and I will not forget the covenant we made when you first came to Me. It is the enemy of your soul that would come to accuse Me in your heart, saying I have forgotten you and your requests. But I remind you, My cherished one, that I can never forget. I carry the marks of the nails every day. This very day a new grace to enter into My faithfulness is being offered to you. Rest in that grace and watch Me work.

✛

CHAPTER 10

THE WILDERNESS: WHERE SONS BECOME SOLDIERS

A re you ready to be molded? The hand of God is continually molding His people. We pass from a wilderness to an oasis of peace and rest only to be prepared for the next wilderness. It is interesting that the next wilderness the Israelites had to pass through was called "the Desert of Sin." Let's take up the story from Exodus 16:

> The whole Israelite community set out from Elim and came to the Desert of Sin, which is between Elim and Sinai. (v. 1)

Actually, the Hebrew word for "Desert of Sin" is not the word for sin or evil, but the word for clay. *A wilderness of clay!* This is the place where we are shaped and molded by the Master Potter. In this wilderness, sons will become soldiers. How did one million slaves become the mighty army of God? Only hardships could turn sons into soldiers. Ask the marines! They can tell you about the crucible they had to pass through in order to become marines. God's preparation is no less thorough.

Exodus 12:51 states, "On that very day the LORD brought the people of Israel out of the land of Egypt like an army."

The delivered must go through more deliverance, a deliverance from complacency and passivity. God knew that they needed to be trained to face the battle conditions that were ahead. Thus far, they had been sheltered. The Hebrews had not fought any battles, yet they were about to go into a land of giants to dislodge them from their strongholds. Cowards would never survive these battles. Only the army of God would be able to prevail against these gates of hell.

It takes a wilderness to shake the complacency and complaining out of us and train us for war. To live victoriously means we must endure hardships and prevail by grace over every difficulty. We must overcome the pain and fear of pressing on into the land of promise.

WHEN GOD SQUEEZED ME

Our journey brought us into a place of being pressed like clay in the hands of God. Shortly after moving into our jungle village of Pucuro as church planters, we began to feel the isolation and pressure of being in an unfamiliar land. It seemed as though the entire village was mocking us and our God.

One evening during a drunken fiesta in the village, I (Brian) lay awake through the night, praying for the people to come to the light of Christ. At about three in the morning, I heard voices outside the door of our hut—angry voices. As I listened, I heard their curses and threats, but as I arose from bed to see who was cursing us, there was no one there! No, it wasn't my imagination—the demon powers in our village were outside our hut, hurling their insults and disgust at our presence in their domain. They wanted us out and were taunting me as I prayed for the village. Their threats were real, but so was God's peace that washed over me that night.

On another occasion we were forced to do battle in prayer as "soldiers in the war" when our precious Joy was bitten by a Bushmaster, a venomous snake, while she was playing on the banks of our jungle river. The Bushmaster's venom is deadly. Many in our village said she would be gone within hours!

As we prayed over her in our hut, a massive hoard of stinging ants came up from underneath her bed and began to swarm all over the floor. Not a good thing! I scooped her up in my arms and took her to another spot in our hut where we could continue our prayer for a miracle.

It seemed in just a moment that things went from bad to worse. Praying in Jesus' name, we had stirred up a hornets' nest, literally! A swarm of hornets appeared out of nowhere in the room and filled the air. At that point, there was no doubt that we were in a struggle of greater proportions than we could have ever imagined. A five-foot-long Bushmaster snake, biting ants, and stinging hornets—this wasn't what we'd envisioned when we answered the missionary call! We felt like we were definitely wrestling with tremendous demonic powers that were trying to remove us from our mission by taking the life of our daughter.

With our hearts clinging to a promise from the Word of God, we prayed out loud this Bible verse:

This is how faithful God will be to you: He will screen and filter the severity, nature, and timing of every test or trial you face—so that you can bear it and walk through it. He will also provide a grace-escape so that you stand up against every hard thing that comes your way. (1 Corinthians 10:13)

As we claimed that verse, we spoke out loud: "Lord, You promised us that You would never allow something into our lives that we would not be able to bear. This is it! Lord, we can't bear this! You have to work a miracle." And He did!

God wonderfully proved that He is faithful! As we prayed, both the ants and the plague of hornets disappeared. Our prayer was answered at daybreak when our mission's airplane flew in, unannounced and unscheduled, to our village. We were able to fly Joy out to a hospital so she could get the medical care she so desperately needed. Joy survived the snakebite as a miracle of grace. Our God is a God who will mold us through our hardships but will never leave us without miracle power. Ask our daughter Joy. She knows firsthand!

What wilderness do you find yourself in today? Is it a place of feeling isolated, even abandoned? Does it seem like the days passing by are taking you no closer to your destiny and the fulfillment of your prophetic promises? Could it be that the hand of the Potter is upon you right now to shape you into a mighty champion: one who will never give up and never quit?

GOD'S WHISPER

I will not let you lose your way! I have led you through many difficult seasons and demonstrated to you My miracle power. Even if you are blind, I will become new eyes to you. Even if you are lame, I will be great strength to you. I will not allow you to wander any longer. When weakness causes you to stumble, I will swiftly run to pick you up and place you even farther on your path. The darkness will become light in front of you, and I will make your steps firm and secure. No matter how well you see Me, I am there to uphold you. No matter how clearly you perceive Me, I will not let you lose your way. I will lead you to the oasis of My presence, and you will be refreshed for your journey. This day I have decreed new eyes and great strength into your life.

✥

CHAPTER 11

THE WILDERNESS: WHY WASTE A GOOD ONE?

One of the great lessons we've learned in the wilderness season is this: disappointment is short-lived. Now, when we're disappointed with God's plan for our lives, we just have to wait a little while longer until we begin to see its purpose and, eventually, its value. God has never wasted a sorrow, heartache, a difficulty, or a trial in our lives. Our great disappointment is not in God but in our impatience and dullness of heart to trust and believe.

One of our early tests in the jungle was when we picked up our children from our mission school and took them with us into our jungle village for their summer break. Our mission plane had been grounded by the government of Panama because they thought that we were CIA agents, so we had to take a long canoe trip into the jungle. We had no idea what was ahead for us. We had no idea that the Chucanaque River that threads through the Darien province of Panama is known for unpredictable floods. One moment the river can be smooth and placid, and the next, the rains upriver can cause it to violently overflow its banks. We were making the trip with Charity, our oldest daughter, who was only seven, Joy, who was six, and David, our infant, who was only five months old.

As we loaded supplies and our kids into a narrow dug-out canoe, we noticed that upriver storm clouds were forming. It had already begun to rain, but we set off into the river anyway with our native guide, as we were anxious to get to our jungle home with the kids. Then suddenly, without warning, we were struck by a rushing wave caused by a massive, spontaneous flood. It was like a tsunami had instantly picked up our canoe and flipped it over! We were all thrown into the rushing river that was now driving us backward. And the river was full of downed trees, destroyed houses, and all kinds of debris that was wildly rushing downriver alongside us. It was like an amusement park ride minus the amusement!

We managed to place all of our children, including our five-month-old, on top of the overturned canoe. There we were, clinging for our lives to the swamped and slippery canoe as we cried out for help in our limited Spanish: "¡Ayúdanos! ¡Ayúdanos!"

Angels in the Wilderness

In a flash, we saw men in small canoes emerging from the banks of the river. Paddling with all their strength, they were coming out amongst the rapids and dangerous debris to rescue us. We believe this was an angelic host, a heavenly response team sent out by God to answer our cry. They lifted us out of the waters one by one and took us ashore. Candice and the children were taken to shore in one place and Brian another. Separated from each other along the banks of the river, we each prayed and asked the Lord to watch over us and reunite our family.

Later that day, all five of us were reunited, and we embraced as we rejoiced in God's goodness. God had rescued us! We will never forget that day and our joyous reunion as the Lord performed a miracle for us. We were alive and we did not drown! We thanked the Lord for sparing our lives and that we still had an opportunity to finish the work God had called us to. We were not disappointed that God had allowed us to face the flooding river, nor that we had lost all our supplies for the next three months of living in the jungle. Rather we gave thanks. It only made us more resilient to go back in.

God is so faithful! Not only were we spared, but He used the whole incident to show our village His love. What a redeeming Father! When we finally arrived at our village and recounted the ordeal back to our new Kuna friends, we will never forget how they just stared at us for the longest time, wondering why we had come back. They wondered why we would still want to stay and live with them instead of going back to *Merki-neg* (America). Years later, when many in our village had turned to Christ, they pointed back to that incident. They told us they knew when we returned to the village after the accident that God had sent us to them, because we didn't turn back and leave them like they had expected. They realized that God had spared our lives so we could deliver the message of life to them.

We want to encourage you to never give up or grow impatient in your hour of distress or peril. If you find yourself in a wilderness, know this: it's to make you strong, not bitter. If you wait in a wilderness long enough, your God will deliver you. He takes note of your heart and listens to your cry. He will not fail to come and rescue the one that He delights in.

> Because you have delighted in me as my great lover, I have chosen to greatly protect you. I will set you in a high place safe and secure before my face. I will answer your cry for help every time you pray, and you will find and feel my presence even in your time of pressure and trouble. I will be your glorious Hero and give you success! (Psalm 91:14–15)

The wilderness of clay has much to teach us. If we fail to be molded by the Master, He may pass us over and succeed with another generation. This is what happened with the Hebrews: in the desert (this "wilderness of clay") was when "the whole community grumbled against Moses and Aaron" (Exodus 16:2).

In our desert days, God is working behind the scenes daily to bring our hearts to faith and stamina, training us for battle. But more often than not, we run from God while we grumble and complain. Most often we grumble against our human leaders, but deep within, we're really bitter at God. The wilderness only exposes our pain and disappointment with the fathering of God.

The experiences of the Israelites teach us so many good lessons about God and His ways. As we see their failures, we begin to see our own. As we learn the lessons they failed to learn, we hasten His progress in our own hearts. It makes it easier for us as we make our journey toward Christlikeness.

Has complaining become a way of life for you? Has the wilderness of clay begun to squeeze you into an uncomfortable place? Let's not fail to learn the lessons God has set before us while we're there!

DON'T WASTE A GOOD WILDERNESS

Many contemporary Christians are inclined to think that those who are spiritual live their lives by "mountaintop experiences," and they feel that a continual spiritual euphoria is required in order to walk in a realm of victory and joy. But Paul and Silas were men of a different breed. While in chains with their bodies battered and bruised, they rejoiced and praised God in the midnight darkness.

God will not allow us to live on endless mountaintops. He has destined us for glory, a glory that comes through many trials, tests, and toils. Adversity brings maturity. This is why the north winds of adversity are necessary for God's growth plan for the believer (Song of Songs 4:16). Trials and tests are fertilizer for the soul. Can you ask the Lord for the wilderness winds? They only come to make you strong!

We find it so interesting that God didn't tell Moses ahead of time about the forty-year period of the wilderness. In essence God told him, "I'll take you out, and I'll lead you in." It was the in-between time that God didn't explain!

There are times He doesn't fill in the blanks; He simply leads you to an in-between place and keeps you there until Christ's life and nature emerges from within you. He reaches His loving hands into the substance of your inner nature and squeezes, forms, and shapes you into a replica of Christ. He will use the in-between place to do His great work of shaping you into the beautiful image of His Son.

Be assured that the place of testing and humiliation is not where God leaves us. The end with the Lord is mercy and grace (James 5:11). Just ask Job! God will not crush us, for Jesus was crushed in our place. Jesus will lift up the bruised reed and fan into flame the smoking embers (Isaiah 42:3). The Lord is tender even in the trials that come to us. If we will seek Him in our weakness, we will learn about mercy like never before. When the test is over, we will find that God is there and that He was so kind to us, really kind!

Another lesson learned in our wilderness season was this: God does not count our failure as a failure unless we allow ourselves to be stuck there. It's also important to note that a continuing state of being stuck in failure will lead to a habit of unbelief and disobedience that will eventually bring you to a dead end. Only you can determine what you'll do with your life. God forgives, guides, instructs, and corrects you, but you are the one who determines if you will stay stuck in the past or move into the triumph of Christ.

Perhaps the closer you get to your conquest, the tougher the training becomes. It may seem like you're going from one wilderness to another with no oasis in between. Those who walk beside us will soon see our failures and our issues. But God's everlasting grace is our hope and true strength. We made a vow years ago that we would never waste any wilderness nor turn back in unbelief like many of our ancestors did … but if He would just draw us, pulling our hearts closer to Him, we would run after Him to the end. Are you ready to make that vow too?

DESERT WARFARE

When you're in the wilderness, it seems like spiritual warfare grows more and more intense. Jesus was led into the wilderness to face the testing and temptation of the devil. There were more demons coming against Christ in that wilderness than you and I could have ever imagined. All of hell was focused on stopping the Son of God from fulfilling His purpose in coming to earth. And so the devil and demons will fight you and tempt you sorely as you get closer to fulfilling your purpose and destiny. The closer you are to the threshold of breakthrough, the hotter the warfare becomes.

David's wilderness experience in the Desert of Judah was pretty rough. He was probably thinking, *I don't look like a king, and I don't feel like a king. What kind of kingdom is this?* And as he was chased by a demonized leader, he could only cry out to heaven and learn firsthand the lessons of spiritual warfare.

We see in Psalm 63:1 the intensity of the wilderness warfare he faced; he said, "O God of my life, I'm lovesick for you in this weary wilderness. I thirst with the deepest longings to love you more with cravings in my heart that can't be described. Such yearning grips my soul for you, my God!"

We have to seek God early, thirst for His presence when we are dry, and not give up when all the outward signs seem to indicate defeat—this is what describes wilderness warfare. There is no hint of revival, no special meeting, and no sense of the presence of God. There's just a passionate, seeking heart that finds grace in the wilderness.

Not only is Jesus an expert when it comes to dealing with demons, He also provides for us in the wilderness when it is dry and there's no water: "Look! I'm about to do something I've never done before! It will spring up right in front of your eyes—can't you recognize what I'm doing? I will open up streams in the desert and paths through the wilderness" (Isaiah 43:19).

Did you know that sometimes a river flows with more than water? Sometimes it flows with grace. If we will but receive it, God will pour it on us like a river of blessing. At times, when we're in the wilderness, it's tempting to rebel and throw in the towel. Even when God shows up and makes us an offer of grace, we seldom go for it. We're usually not looking for grace—we're looking for a fast train out! We just want out! But David perse-vered in the wilderness. This proved his character. You can see this pictured in what Paul the apostle taught when he said:

> But that's not all! Even in times of trouble we have a joy-ful confidence, knowing that our pressures develop in us patient endurance. And patient endurance will refine our character, and proven character leads us back to hope. (Romans 5:3–4)

Why not keep a journal? You're going to learn so many fan-tastic truths about God in the coming days. God is providing everything you need to become like His Son. His care for you includes meeting every need, even in a wilderness. Yes, keep a journal. It may become your own book on your wilderness experiences!

GOD'S WHISPER

Though a flood overtakes you, I will lift you high. Though fires burn around you, I will be Your shelter. Though many voices may speak to accuse, I will be Your peace. Haven't I saved you a thousand times? You see but one, but I see the many times I have rescued you, sheltered you, covered you, and protected you from your folly. Take rest in your Father's works. Take joy in your Father's love. This day I will open your eyes to see My salvation in your life. The day of the Redeemer has come. My redeeming grace will be unveiled before you. This is the day that I will arise to redeem your life and restore it fully back to Me. From today forward My presence will be upon your life in unmistakable ways. My face will lead your steps and protect you from all that may come against you. Though a raging flood threatens you, I will lift you high, and you will see My glory, for the day of the Redeemer has come!

❖

CHAPTER 12

THE WILDERNESS: A PLACE OF SATISFACTION AND CONVICTION

D o you ever complain? I mean, really. Do you ever just find yourself so grumpy and disappointed with life that you wish someone else could live it for you? The good news is that the bad news makes us hungry for the good news. Jesus can take our place and fight our battles! Every wilderness will take us to a fresh discovery of our all-sufficient Christ!

Take a moment and join me on the journey to find the place of the miraculous power of God. But you have to settle your heart once and for all, that no matter what, you won't turn back. You will not be one who gives up only to spend your life as a grumbler in your wilderness.

Where do miracles originate? Is there really a place where a miracle is born? Let's find out! But we need to warn you—it won't be where you expect. It might not be on a platform or in a meeting or in having someone pray for you.

My dear fellow believers, I don't want you to be unaware that all our Jewish ancestors who walked through a wilderness long ago were under the glory cloud, and passed through the waters of the sea on both sides. They were all baptized into the cloud of glory, into the fellowship of Moses, and into the sea. They all ate the same heavenly manna and drank water from the same spiritual rock that was coming with them—and that Rock was Christ himself. (1 Corinthians 10:1-4)

So the journey of the Israelites is a picture of the journey of the believer into the Promised Land of the fullness of Christ. Everything that happened to the Hebrews is an example of what happens to us as we move forward into our calling. The ups and downs of the wilderness trek are an experience that all of us are familiar with. We experience miracles and dramatic answers to prayer only to be thrust into new and unexpected difficulties.

During our wilderness days here on earth, the delight of Father God is to lead us from the natural into the supernatural, from the earthly into the heavenly realms. It's the thin place between two kingdoms. It's the thin place that you can walk in and out of daily. Lord, take us to that thin place!

This is seen so clearly as God, the Provider, gives spiritual food to His people. Only a supernatural supply can satisfy the people of God. He rains down bread from heaven as a sign of His loving provision. God opens up a rock and pours out water to satisfy the thirsting soul. Jesus is both living bread and living water.

You sent your living breath, your sweet Spirit, to give them understanding. All during their journey you never failed to give them your miracle bread from heaven and miracle water to quench their thirst! (Nehemiah 9:20)

Despite the miracle of the Red Sea, the continual covering of the glory cloud, the bitter waters sweetened by a tree, and the refreshment of Elim, the people were still in a grumbling mood. They ventured out into a wilderness called Sin ("the wilderness of clay") between Elim, the place of bubbling springs, and Sinai, the place where they were destined to meet God and enter into a covenant relationship with Him. They were in a transition place. Have you ever been there? Maybe even at this moment you are facing a transition in your life and are in a place between a memory of mercy and a destiny so distant.

Can you see how the Israelites' story parallels your life? God delivers you from your past, yet He keeps bringing you to a place of impossibility where you're forced to trust Him for your future. And this happens over and over. You're brought to a bitter place of pain, yet the healing tree of Calvary makes it sweet. These experiences are not God's punishment but His instruction. He's preparing us to sit and rule with His Son for all eternity as His loving bride at His side!

To change what we are in the flesh will take a wilderness, a desert that exposes all that's hidden inside of us: "In the desert the whole community grumbled against Moses and Aaron" (Exodus 16:2 NIV). God wants to expose and deal with everything in the wilderness that prevents us from living like Christ. The people grumbled because of a lack of nourishment. Our true supply and nourishment is the life of Christ. When we're not satisfied with feeding each moment on His heavenly life, we end up complaining and full of negativity. When Christ fills us, He satisfies us, and His abundant life overflows within and conquers our complaining flesh life.

Deep within, most believers today are undernourished in the supply of Christ as their daily bread. We are undernourished in feeding our inner man with Christ. Doctrines and duties just won't do it. We have to have the Living Bread from heaven, the mystery Manna Man who satisfies.

The Israelites essentially said to Moses, "If only we had died by the Lord's hand in Egypt! At least when we were there, we sat around pots of meat and ate all the food we wanted, but you've brought us out into this desert to starve this entire assembly."

How soon they had forgotten both their insufferable bondage and how wonderfully God had delivered them! So they began to accuse Moses and Aaron of bringing them into the wilderness on some death march. When we forget where we've come from, it is easy to complain.

Growling Stomachs and Grumbling Lips

The word *grumble* occurs nine times in Exodus 16. So let's consider the truth about grumbling: grumbling is a problem of perception. When we grumble and complain, we lose perspective and distort our perception of what's happening. Israel was being tested by God to be prepared to witness a heavenly miracle—the provision of manna. It wasn't to destroy them but to disciple them into God's ways. We often exaggerate our problems and underestimate the power of God to deliver us. The problem of perception results in a complaining, negative mood that blinds us to God's true purpose, which is to make us more like Christ.

Grumbling is a problem of submission. When we grumble, we are saying, *I don't like God's direction for my life and will not submit to this test.* The Hebrews complained against Moses and Aaron, not realizing that it was really God who was leading them by a glory cloud over their heads. Let's face it, we're unable to see the Lord as He truly is when we're complaining about His ways.

Grumbling is a problem with self-control. Our hearts bleed through our speech. Our tongues begin to vent what's in our heart. If only we would listen to what we're saying, we'd realize what we've been feeding on. It's a sin to complain and murmur our way through life, for our tongues were created to praise the Lord in all things.

Grumbling is a virus, a communicable disease that is highly contagious. How quickly one complaining heart multiplies into many! We're told that the "whole community" began to grumble. No doubt it was really only a few voices that spread the epidemic of negativity throughout the whole congregation.

Grumbling is a demonstration of our lack of faith. Unbelief blinds our eyes to God's goodness all around us. We begin to see our problems through our doubts rather than through the eyes of faith, knowing there is no impossible situation with God. Faith says God is bigger than any problem we may have and there is no problem He is unable to fix. But grumbling says this problem is an exception—and I may die waiting for Him to come to my rescue! Faith always looks beyond the momentary mess and sees a miracle in the making. Even a miracle can be seen in the wilderness.

If you were God, how would you respond to a million grumblers? Amazingly, God says, *I know how I'll fix this. They just need to see my glory!* Seeing the glory of God is the answer to a negative heart. The Lord knew that the Hebrews were mere children in the ways of God. They had so much to learn. As a merciful Father He showed them mercy, not judgment. God was not coming to kill them, but to feed them. And even as they complained, the glory cloud was providing refreshing shade over their heads. He will never stop being faithful to His people.

One sight of glory will cure you of your grumbling. We know that when we're complaining and whining and inviting others to our pity party, we're not focused on the glory cloud that is above us and within us. If we can see His beautiful glory, full of all that we need and all that we want, we will be delivered from grumbling. And we will come up out of our wilderness leaning on our Beloved.

A baptism of glory is coming to cure us and to make us like Christ. Can you see His glory? There was a time in the wilderness when the glory of God actually became food for His people. Every morning for forty years, a miracle took place as food fell down from heaven. Miracles will do it every time! Our grumbling goes away when we see the unmistakable breakthrough of power and when we're convinced that God is with us after all.

One of the greatest miracles we have ever witnessed was the dramatic conversion of hundreds of precious Kuna people in our village of Pucuro. We had spent too much time complaining about their lack of desire to hear *Pab igal* (God's Word) and not enough time praying in faith for the breakthrough. Then one day it seemed like we'd had enough. We felt empty and discouraged; we had reached our limit and had no more strength to carry on.

One night we lay in our bed, under our mosquito net, praying with tears and asking God to break through for us and shake our village with His power. We begged God to open the hearts of the people we had come to reach with the gospel. We said to God, "Lord, if You don't come through and work a miracle of grace and open their hearts to the gospel, we're going back home to the United States. We'll have to tell the people who supported us that You were not great enough to conquer their strongholds of unbelief and pride. God, You *must* break through in this situation and bring a move of heavenly power to this village!" It was a bold prayer—a prayer challenge that God was more than able to answer.

The next morning, we could feel a shift in the atmosphere over our jungle village. Something was up—as if God's presence was hovering over the village that morning! But what happened next forever changed us.

God broke through, but His breakthrough began first in us. We began to feel our sin of unbelief that the people could be saved, and Brian began to feel his own sin of anger against the people he was sent to love. We could feel the weight of God's Holy Spirit convicting our hearts.

I (Brian) decided I needed to humble myself before the Lord.

I (Candice) had had my own "come to Jesus" moment earlier during our daughter's snakebite experience.

Now it was my (Brian's) turn as tears began to pour down my face, and I humbled my heart before the Father. And the Lord revealed to me that I was the reason we hadn't seen the breakthrough. I was the proud one, the very stumbling block keeping others from coming to know God. The Lord showed me that the problem was in my heart, and that I was wanting everyone around me to change instead of allowing the Lord to change me first.

As the morning sun rose over our village, the trail of tears began. I decided I would go to every hut in the village and ask everyone to forgive me for my lack of love and my impatience, anger, and poor example of Jesus Christ before their eyes. As my tears mingled with their tears, they received me as a friend. A miracle took place that day as a mighty revival swept through Pucuro.

As the day ended and I finished my "repentance journey," God's Spirit fell. People were weeping and broken as the deep convicting work of the Spirit of God began to pour out. It was the beginning of true revival, the breakthrough we had prayed for!

A true move of God came when I stopped complaining and began confessing my deep need for more of Jesus. As a result, the Kuna people were forever changed that day. The church of Pucuro was birthed out of a move of repentance sweeping through—and it all began with a move of God in my needy heart first.

What about you, friend? Are you too busy grumbling over the godlessness of those around you? Have you forgotten to repent over your own sin? Everything around you will change when you break open your heart and allow the presence of Jesus to flood you deep inside. God is ready to break open the heavens when you're ready to allow Him to have His way with your heart.

GOD'S WHISPER

Bring your heart before Me, and I will deepen your love. To love others seems so difficult when you are distant and detached from My presence. When I draw near to you, love is born. Everything that would dilute the power of My love disappears when I am near. Love flows from My presence and reaches, like a river, to the lowest place. The omnipotence of My love will conquer the fear and doubt that hides in your heart. Bring your heart closer to Me, and I will deepen your love.

The process I have taken you through is only so that My love will be greater than your disappointment. Many react to the difficulties of life out of a heart filled with pain. I promise you, My love will win the day if you will turn to Me when others walk away. A great education is not enough to transfer My love into your heart. A brilliant mind will not be sufficient to carry a love that surpasses understanding. Human logic will always leave you empty when you stand before the fire of My love.

My flame needs no fuel, nothing of man, for it is a self-replenishing fire. I will bring you deeper into My ways as the fire burns up all that hinders love. Bring your heart before Me now, and I will take you to the place where love is born.

✤

CHAPTER 13

THE WILDERNESS: WHERE MANNA RAINS DOWN

Everyone we know struggles with something. It may be God's delay in bringing you into your full destiny or God's ways in teaching you wisdom. Our problems are unique to each one of us, but this we know for certain: "Even when bad things happen to the good and godly ones, the Lord will save them and not let them be defeated by what they face" (Psalm 34:19).

It's okay to admit it. Our afflictions can be both strange and hard to take. We often resent the way God leads us and the paths we end up walking to find our Destiny Road. Many will get angry when they don't get their way and forget that "every detail of our lives is continually woven together to fit into God's perfect plan of bringing good into our lives" (Romans 8:28).

In the face of their complaining, the Lord gave the Hebrews a revelation of who He really was. And He showed them a miracle!

The greatest healing of the heart came in the glory cloud as the manna began to fall out of heaven!

Then the Lord Yahweh said to Moses, "Because of you, I will rain down bread from the heavenly realm. The people must go out each day and gather enough for that day. This will be a test for them to see if they will faithfully follow my instructions. On every sixth day they will gather twice as much as on the other days, and tell them to prepare all that they bring in" (Exodus 16:4–5).

Instead of raining down fire and brimstone as punishment for their murmuring, the gracious God of Israel rained down mercy and manna. Like a father who loves His children, God provided food for His household. But they were tested each day to see if they would believe God to feed them (Deuteronomy 8:3, 16). God will reduce you, too, to the place where you need him daily: the place of humility.

We will never feed upon Christ if we still have our own provision. If we see ourselves as full and needing nothing, even the treasures of Christ will seem to be insignificant to us. Hunger will open our souls to the source of a satisfying life, Christ within. The place of stripping is where we see our need the way God sees it, and we discover Christ as the complete answer for every need. Humility and hunger are both born in the wilderness.

WONDER BREAD

The promise of "Wonder Bread" from heaven was also a test! God was testing them through this miracle to see if they would walk in His instruction. This same test is given to us today. He will test us with miracles to see if we will steward that miracle with humility and faithfulness, obeying His voice. Will we get up first thing every morning to gather our "spiritual manna"? Fresh revelation is our daily bread, our very strength. God will rain it down from heaven if we care enough every morning to gather it and feast upon it!

Do you know anything that smells better than fresh bread? It has a way of making us instantly hungry. When we feed upon Him as our manna, we take in the fresh and tasty bread of heaven. It fills us with the very ingredients of heaven, making us ready and eager to share it with others. This passion will then cause others to want more of this bread too. And the cycle will continue, releasing a desire within you to give Him your heart each and every morning. This is true humility: seeking God above all other desires!

God is so bored with our grumbling. It wearies Him. But He has a way of steering our hearts from pain into His pleasure. No one else has the cure for complaining like He does! How does He do it? The murmuring of a million people was interrupted by a miracle!

> As Aaron was still speaking to the people, they looked to the desert and suddenly the glory of the Lord Yahweh appeared over the desert, manifested in a cloud! And the Lord Yahweh said to Moses, "I have heard all the grumbling of the Israelites. Tell them this: 'At sunset you will eat all the meat you want, and tomorrow morning you will be filled with bread. Then you will know that I am Lord Yahweh, your God.'" (Exodus 16:10–12)

The Lord spoke out of His glory cloud and told His people they were not forgotten. It was out of the glory that they would be fed. The miracle they needed and the miracle you need today is found right over your life—in the cloud of His glorious presence.

There is bread in the glory for you! The heart of every believer should be ready to receive the bread of glory. Not just barely enough, but enough to be filled even to overflowing. Miracles have nutrients. Glory has substance. Just as there are nutrients in food, there is a satisfying and filling experience full of nutrients called *miracles*. Are you extracting from your miracles the nutrients of God? He will work a miracle in our lives simply to impart the bread of His glory into our inner being.

The word for *manna* in the Hebrew means "What is it?" Your Father loves to feed you with mystery bread! You wonder where it comes from, you wonder what it means, you wonder why this is the way He feeds you, and admit it—you wonder why you have to be in a wilderness to see this miracle! Makes you wonder, doesn't it?

Angels' Food Fell from the Sky

Still he spoke on their behalf and the skies opened up;
the windows of heaven poured out food,
the mercy bread-manna.
The grain of grace fell from the clouds.
Humans ate angels' food, the meal of the mighty ones.
His grace gave them more than enough!
(Psalm 78:23–25)

Isn't that awesome! Men ate the bread of angels! Angel food cake was served by heavenly caterers daily. No one had to work for it; they didn't have to grind the flour and knead the dough or bake it over the fire. It came ready to eat. No more devil's food cake for you! It's time to eat the mystery manna of the angels! What is it? Yes, we're still asking, "What is it?"

It is Jesus! The manna that fell from heaven points us to the true Bread of Life, Jesus Christ. The manna came out of the glory cloud and fell to the earth. So did Jesus Christ. He came out of the realm of glory and landed on the earth as the Son of God to become the Son of Man. Jesus Christ is the Wonder Bread from heaven!

Jesus one day fed five thousand hungry people with an endless supply of bread from five small loaves (Mark 6:38). Just as God supplied food for the Hebrews in the wilderness, Jesus gave the hungry a meal of bread and fish. The people looked to Jesus to become a meal ticket for them for the rest of their lives. He fed a multitude in the wilderness and is still able to feed me.

Jesus stood before them and multiplied the bread to demonstrate He was the God who sustained the weary tribes of Israel in their wilderness journey. The miracle of bread was the forty-year miracle of manna pushed into one day! His touch released the glory as the bread they broke grew back. The fish they shared multiplied! Everything multiplies when Jesus holds it in His glorious hands. If we only knew who it is that cares for us, our troubles would take a vacation.

Listen to what Jesus told them:

They replied, "Show us a miracle so we can see it, and then we'll believe in you. Moses took care of our ancestors who were fed by the miracle of manna every day in the desert, just like the Scripture says, 'He fed them with bread from heaven.' What sign will you perform for us?"

"The truth is," Jesus said, "Moses didn't give you the bread of heaven. It's my Father who offers bread that comes as a dramatic sign from heaven. The bread of God is the One who came out of heaven to give his life to feed the world."

"Then please, sir, give us this bread every day," they replied.

Jesus said to them, "I am the Bread of Life. Come

every day to me and you will never be hungry. Believe in me and you will never be thirsty." (John 6:30–35)

Jesus Christ feeds the spirit. He fills and satisfies the yearnings of the human heart. Each of us has a breadbasket inside that is meant to be filled with Jesus, not the things of the flesh. Twelve baskets full—one for each disciple—still remains! If you would be satisfied with the crumbs from His table, imagine what a basketful would do for you! Each of us has a breadbasket full of the life-giving fragments of Jesus. Even a fragment can fill you up! There is a supernatural supply of life that is our daily bread: "Give us each day what is needed for that day" (Luke 11:3).

Are you feeding your heart on Him today? If you are, then you'll have to be content feeding on mystery. Taste and see that the Lord is good and satisfying, even when you're not able to answer fully, "What is it?"

Imagine what it was like looking every day for "What is it?" Can you picture the Hebrews going out of their tents in the morning and saying, "What is this stuff? What in the world is it?" You can almost hear a Hebrew mother telling her kids to go out and gather some "What is it?" for breakfast. "Right, Mom, but what is it?"

In the morning there was a layer of dew covered the ground around the camp. When the dew evaporated there appeared thin flakes like frost on the desert floor. And when the Israelites saw it, they looked at each other and said, "What is it?" For they didn't have a clue what it was. But Moses said to them, "It's the bread from heaven the Lord Yahweh has given you to eat" … So the people of Israel called the bread "manna." It was white like coriander seed and tasted like wafers made with honey. (Exodus 16:13–15, 31)

This mystery meal is called "God's manna" in Nehemiah 9:20. It is called "heaven's bread" in Psalm 105:40 and "angels' food" in Psalm 78:25. It is our true "heavenly manna" in 1 Corinthians 10:3. Mystery manna! God feeds us with mystery. We all want answers, sometimes more than God is wanting to share them with us. We want to know in advance the GPS route through our wilderness, but God's positioning system is a secret. We don't always know where we're going and how we'll get there. That's our food for today. We feed our curiosity not on insisting God tells us what we want to know, but in stilling our soul like a "weaned child."

Listen to David's heart:

Lord, my heart is meek before you.
I don't consider myself better than others.
I'm content to not pursue matters
That are over my head—
Such as your complex mysteries and wonders—
that I'm not yet ready to understand.
I am humbled and quieted in your presence.
Like a contented child that rests on its mother's lap,
I'm your resting child,
and my soul is content in you.
(Psalm 131:1–2)

"Contented" children will simply rest and not demand food, crying until they get it. A "contented child" knows the food is coming. God's way to satisfy you is through the mystery of His ways! His ways may puzzle you, but they will also perfect you.

GOD'S WHISPER

I won't send you away hungry. When you come to Me for more, you receive all that you desire. Did not I feed five thousand hungry ones until they were satisfied? I will fill you five thousand times over with My Living Bread, the life found in Me. You will not lack one good thing, for I've given you all of My heart. It's the hungry that are satisfied; it's the lowly that are lifted high; it's the desperate that discover; and it's the passionate that will find My pleasure. I'll not send you away hungry, so come this day and find even more than you desire.

✤

THE WILDERNESS:
WHERE FAITH IS TESTED

F aith doesn't grow in a greenhouse but in a wilderness. The wilderness is the special place where God takes you aside to rekindle divine romance, upgrade your identity, and expand your faith. Many great things God is famous for began in a wilderness. Moses came from the wilderness to deliver the Jews, Joshua to conquer the Promised Land, John the Baptist to reveal Jesus, and Jesus came out of His wilderness to redeem the world.

Faith is something that must be fed and nourished. It can grow stronger with the right nutrients. So what are the right types of nutrients for growing strong faith? It may surprise you, but faith thrives on difficulty and testing. The trial of your faith will bring a greater dimension of God into your soul. Faith tested will be faith growing!

The food for your faith is the difficulty you're facing right now. Eat your difficulty—gobble it up and watch it disappear. This was the lesson of the hour for the Israelites. They were given food from heaven to help them overcome the fear of life in the wilderness. God feeds us with just what we need to grow strong and more like Christ. Instead of cutting out all problems from your life, God will cut out your doubts by making your faith muscle even stronger so that you're able to overcome.

In every adversity we have two options: we can run away and escape, or we can accept our circumstances as a challenge to triumph. Victories are never won by running from the battle. Victories are won by standing in faith and believing the truth that "I can endure all things through Christ who strengthens me" (Philippians 4:13).

What about the Hebrew people as they endured their lengthy trek through one wilderness after another? God was faithful to them even when they doubted and even when they complained. We're convinced that one of the greatest miracles of all time was the miracle of manna rain falling each morning to feed more than one million people for nearly forty years in the desert! Let's start with looking at how manna is described in Exodus 16.

1. Manna was sweet like honey.

We think of it like frosted flakes that fell every morning, full of nutrients and sweetness. How pleasant this must have been to scoop up this sweet bread, with the taste of honey that had just fallen from the sky. We know that honey in the Bible often speaks of the revelation of Christ. The Word of Christ is like revelation honey to our lips. The sweetness of heaven fell every morning for breakfast. There is none as sweet to the soul as Jesus Christ (Song of Songs 1:3).

2. Manna fell fresh every day.

Jesus is ever fresh and ever new to the heart who feeds on

Him. Nothing stale, outdated, or moldy. What a joy each day to feed upon this "daily bread." Christ's anointed Word is new for us every day and never fails or runs dry (Lamentations 3:22–23).

3. *Manna tasted as if it had been made with olive oil (Numbers 11:8).*

This olive oil is a picture of the new anointing that rests upon Him. He was pressed in Gethsemane's olive press to provide us with the richness of His Spirit. None of us have an anointing that did not come from Him. He paid the price at Calvary and poured out the oil of His Spirit upon all who love Him. Nothing is more precious that this Living Manna made with olive oil. Take some today!

4. *Manna fell with the dew of the morning (Numbers 11:9).*

To seek Jesus in the early morning yields sweetness to our souls. For our Lord Jesus is anointed with the Holy Spirit without measure. Just as the manna fell very early each morning, so our soul should ache for Him to come to us each and every day as we arise and awaken our soul to feast upon Him. The refreshing "dew of the morning" is waiting for you to bring you strength.

5. *Manna was like coriander seed.*

The coriander is such a tiny seed. It's a seed that has life within. And so it is with Christ: when we eat of Him, He comes into us like a seed and grows within us. To seek Jesus early in the morning, day after day, is like planting a supernatural seed into your spirit. He will increase in you as you feed your heart on Him.

6. *Manna comes from a supernatural food group that is not of this earth.*

Manna means, "What is it?" It's a mystery. It comes from heaven to supply God's people with supernatural life. Every day our hearts are fed by this mystery bread—"What is this? How is it that God satisfies my spirit?" Mystery feeds us. It should be a daily part of life. Western Christians demand answers; God simply wants to feed us out of a realm of not knowing, a realm where there are no answers, only satisfaction.

Every encounter with God in our wilderness should leave us in the place of awe, not answers. Mystery is designed to mess with our heads. The Hebrew phrase, "an omer for each person" (Exodus 16:16) can actually be translated, "an omer for each skull."

We need mystery to somehow penetrate our minds, or our skulls. God delights in overwhelming us until we have to say, "What is it?" If there's not mystery involved in some way, it's probably not God.

Jesus was crucified at Golgatha, "the place of the skull." Look at the Hebrew word for "person" or "skull" in Exodus 16. It's *golgoleth*, which is the word for Golgatha! The cross must be placed over our thoughts and our minds or we'll miss the mystery, the truth of God. That's food for thought! Start feeding yourself on that Wonder Bread and let God keep you wrapped in mystery as He feeds you manna in the wilderness.

A MIRACLE EVERY MORNING

God is definitely a morning person. Don't be mistaken, He works the night shift too, but He really has something special for you each morning. So here's the deal—you have to get up and stoop low and eat it! Come on, sleepyhead, morning miracles are just outside your door!

Manna fell from the sky right in front of their tents. Forget about Snack Packs, this was the real deal! Angels' food falling at their feet! At daybreak the manna was found around the camp. No long journey was required to gather it. It was right at hand. And so it is with Jesus, our Bread of Life. He's accessible, easy to find, and close enough to reach. It was so near that they either had to gather it or trample it beneath their feet. And so it is with Jesus in this hour. We will either take Him to our home and feed our hearts in His sweetness, or we'll walk over His mercies. If we neglect Him and fail to gather our daily bread, we will be ignoring the greatest gift God has ever given us.

Beloved, let's say it clearly: God wants to feed you every morning with Living Bread from heaven! That alone gets us out of bed in the morning hours. It isn't money, food, or anything else. It's the thought that Jesus has left a miracle of manna within reach.

We'll never forget the times when we woke at four in the morning to read our Bibles by the light of a kerosene lamp. Sitting in the jungle with no light switch or gourmet coffee maker, we still found a jar of manna waiting for us. Those were days when Jesus fed us extravagantly. We had no church to attend. We had breakfast before our breakfast. He strengthened us during those long days of learning the language, translating the New Testament Scriptures into the Paya-Kuna dialect, and teaching the people the Word of God. We had to first teach them how to read before we could even give them the New Testament in their language.

It's still refreshing to us years later. He is still our delight early in the morning! You might not be in a jungle or have the best coffee maker, but you can join us each morning in finding that golden jar of manna waiting for you. We love Him like no other, don't you?

Let's find the manna that feeds us. Here are some truths to help you gather your daily bread:

1.   We each must gather our own manna.

This is what the LORD has commanded: "Each one is to gather as much as he wants to eat. Gather an omer for each person you have in your tent." (Exodus 16:16)

No one can gather your daily portion for you. You must be the one that arises and gathers to your spirit your fresh provision of the life and power of Jesus on a daily basis. It's the immature that always have to have someone there to teach them. But the Holy Spirit wants to unveil Jesus to you personally as you wait in the morning before Him. Books are good, but the Author of the Book, the Holy Spirit, is the best!

2.   Manna must be gathered in the early morning.

Every morning the people gathered as much as each one needed, and when the sun grew hot, it would melt away. (Exodus 16:21)

Manna was gathered early, before other things filled their attention. If they waited too long, the heat of the day would cause the manna to melt away. Your daily portion of Christ waits for you with every sunrise. Blessed are those who seek Him early (Proverbs 8:34). The manna of His presence gives you a new and powerful beginning each day. Growth into the fullness of Christ is a daily gathering of His virtue into our inner beings. We must seek our daily bread. Don't let the day's distractions keep you from a holy hour of devotion. Are you finding Him before the sun gets hot?

3. The manna was gathered by stooping low.

With bended knee, the Hebrews would stoop to gather their daily portion. Manna did not grow on trees; rather, it fell on the ground. They didn't need to reach up high, but they had to bow down low. We must humble our hearts and be willing to stoop low in order to find this angels' food for our soul. Come hungry to the Living Bread and you'll be fed. He will never turn you away without giving you your portion.

4. Some gathered more, some gathered less.

The Israelites did as they were told; some gathered a lot, some only a little. And when they measured it by the omer, the one who gathered a lot did not have any to spare, and the one who gathered a little was not left wanting more. Each one gathered as much as he needed. (Exodus 16:17–18)

This is true with us in the body of Christ today. Some are ready each morning to gather as much as they possibly can, while others gather as little as they can to get by. We each gather as much as we need. Are you one who needs a lot from Christ? There is plenty to spare and enough to go around. His life is a fountain that never runs dry.

5. What was gathered must be consumed that day.

Then Moses said to them, "No one should keep any of it until tomorrow." However, some of them ignored Moses' instruction; they kept part of it until morning, but it was ruined, full of maggots, and began to stink. (Exodus 16:20)

We must ask for our daily portion and then arise to seek it out. Truth that's not lived out in the life of a believer eventually begins to smell. You can store away your Bible doctrines on a shelf, but if you don't live them out each day, you may have people avoiding you! I hate to be the one to tell you, but hypocrisy stinks! We will either put on the cologne of Christ or the scent of self-satisfaction. Don't worry about storing up enough to last for two days—yesterday's bread won't cut it! You must feed on Him today as daily bread. You really are what you eat!

As you feed on Him, you actually take this miracle manna into your spirit. Soon you will become a golden jar full of this bread. The church is about to become a golden jar serving Wonder Bread to the nations!

GOD'S WHISPER

I will be food for you. Do not search for that which will not satisfy your soul. Come to Me, and I will be your feast. Day after day I will care for your soul. Rest in My love that provides for you all that is needed—strength for the day and hope for your future. I love you more than any parent can love a child. I will give even more than what you ask for or what you can imagine. Leave what is good for what is best. Come and find true soul-satisfying strength in My love. You are my chosen one, and I will not forget all that you have done for Me and all that you have poured out at My feet. Your love satisfies Me, even as My love delights your heart. Seek Me early and you will find Me.

✤

CHAPTER 15

THE WILDERNESS: WHERE THE WEAK BECOME STRONG

All the tests they had to pass through on their way through the wilderness is a symbolic picture, and example and warning for us. We can learn through what they experienced—for we live in a time when the climax and closing curtain of all the ages past is now completing its goal in us. (1 Corinthians 10:11)

Many people say the desert is where nothing grows. That's simply not true. The desert is fertile ground. It's a land rich with spiritual nutrients to strengthen our spirit and bring true transformation to our lives. We'll grow into the image of Christ in the climate of difficulty.

If you've never experienced a spiritual wilderness, you may have difficulty understanding this chapter. Even some of us who have passed through more than one wilderness may have a difficult time understanding what we are about to say. Let's face it—most of us don't like to consider the wilderness as a part of our Christian journey. Our theology makes little room for great trials. Everyone wants a beach, not a barren wilderness. Right?

But listen, just as God created deserts and wildernesses in His natural creation, He has also designed deserts and wildernesses to fulfill a crucial part of transforming His spiritual creation. Most of us say that our times of dryness and distress come from the devil or our own disobedience. However, the apostle Paul confirmed that the wilderness Israel experienced is also to be a picture of what we'll walk through in our journey toward Christlikeness. The journey of the Hebrews will be the journey of all those destined for rulership.

The actual Hebrew word for *desert* comes from a root word meaning "the place of speaking." Simply stated, the desert is the place where God speaks to us! Some of the greatest messages you receive from God will be spoken to you in your desert difficulty. He will speak in your desert and cause it to blossom like a rose. In the lonely place of isolation, God will speak in a way that you will perceive, and you'll begin to hear His voice clearly. Through the howling wind, the blazing sun, and the scorching sand, God will speak.

Living in a tribal village with barking dogs, crowing roosters, and all the noise associated with communal living made it difficult for us to have a "quiet time" in the morning. Constant interruptions forced us to come up with an alternative so we could quiet our hearts, meditate on the Word of God, and listen to the One who wanted to speak with us.

So here's what we came up with. The men got up very early to go hunting or work in their field and would come over to our house before they went out. So we would just get up earlier, lighting our kerosene lamp to have our time alone with Jesus. Or so we thought! The moment we struck the match to light our lamp, even at 4:30 in the morning, the neighbors would see the light and begin to stream over to our hut. They wanted to ask us questions about *Pab Tummad*, which means in the Kuna language, "Father God."

After several weeks of this, we knew that we had to devise another plan. We felt that ache to be alone in a quiet place to listen to God's voice. So we built a shack a short walk from the village. It was close enough to be available but far enough from the village to be left alone. The people puzzled over why we were putting up a shack out in the jungle. They would hear Brian praying out loud in the shack and thought that he was talking to the animals or to himself. After much explaining, they began to understand that he was speaking to *Pab Tummad*.

Even today, many years later, we're so thankful for the time we spent with Him in the wee hours of the morning out in the jungle. So now, when our hearts become weary with our journey or we lose focus along the way, we can still find the brooks of bliss flowing in His presence. These quiet times are some of the best times of our lives. God draws near as we come close to Him. We wait there silently to hear what He would whisper to our hearts. Weakness turns to strength as we wait upon the Lord. Yes, the wilderness is the place where God speaks. Are you listening for His voice?

Your desert may not be a sandy one, but it can surely be a difficult one. The desert, for you, could be an unfulfilled marriage. It could be an unhealed physical condition that's been prayed for countless times. Or it may be a wayward child or an obstinate coworker. <u>Deserts come in all kinds of sizes.</u> God has a tailor-made wilderness that fits you and one that fits us as well. Your desert will become a sacred spot where self will be laid down in the dust and God alone will be exalted.

While we're in the desert, we have a choice. We can respond with thoughts that say, "What am I doing here? Why me? I don't really need this. Others need to be broken and go through this stuff, but not me." This is the response of a *proud heart* that assumes a spirituality that is not real in our daily lives.

Or we can say, "I'm tired of this! It's gone on long enough! Doesn't God know I'm sick of this stuff?" This is the response of an *unbroken heart* that's still kicking and clawing against the ways of God. The only way this impatience will help us is if it drives us to prayer.

But the third response is to say, "Okay, Lord, You are always right. You know more than I do—I accept this process. You've never made a mistake in guiding my life." This is the only response that reveals a *mature heart*. This response leaves the timing of your release with Abba, because Abba knows best!

This reminds me (Candice) of my employment at a very prestigious business institution. I learned some major life lessons the hard way. They were lessons that were tailor-made to awaken my heart to God. Brian and I were pastoring a growing congregation, but it was taking time, and our income was not great enough to support our family of five. The church was not able to pay for our insurance, so we decided I would seek employment in order to supplement our income and procure insurance for our family.

I started out by working several temporary jobs until I was finally hired on full time with a reputable company that offered wonderful benefits. It was a pure miracle that I got the job. I won't go into all the details, but it was obvious to everyone it was a divine setup because everything fell into place so perfectly. Little did I know, I was entering a three-year wilderness journey!

At the time of my hire, I was still learning how to use a computer. I would spend my evenings teaching myself on a tutorial. It was all so new and foreign to me at the time, but I was determined to learn. Finding a job depended on it. The manager who hired me actually knew I didn't meet all the qualifications that the job required, but she was willing to take a risk on me and said, "Please learn quickly. I need you, as I don't trust any of the other applicants. Our office is in turmoil, and even though your skill set may not be the best, I believe it will improve. Right now I just need someone in the office that I can trust. And I feel like I can trust you."

So basically I was hired on my trustworthiness. But little did I know that the girl sitting in the cubicle next to me had contested my hire. She really wanted my job and took it all the way to the labor union. Unfortunately a labor union doesn't look at your qualifications of trustworthiness. So one week I had a job, and the next week I received a termination letter. She won her case, and I was out. She would replace me in two weeks. You can just imagine how fun it was to work right next to her. She was really ready to get me out of there and tried to sabotage me every day that she waited.

Every day she continued to make my life miserable, hoping that I would mess up so that she could get me out sooner. This was the beginning of my learning to trust God in a whole new way. I longed to be back in the jungle! But God is so God. Within a week, she manifested her true colors and had two meltdowns with managers. Each time she was written up. And then she had a third. That was it! They were done with her. So the boss called the security guards, and they carried her kicking and screaming all the way out the door. And in an instant, I had the job back!

Whew, the battle was over! Or so I thought! Not really. This whole process should have been a sign for me. This was only the beginning of three years of battle. I'll spare you the gory details, only to say I learned how to endure difficulty as a good soldier and to fight the good fight of faith. I had to arm myself for my coworker battles each and every day. The natives in the jungle were easier to work with. The Word of God and prayer were my salvation. I realized my battle was not with flesh and blood but with principalities and powers in high places.

The workplace became my wilderness. But it was there that I learned to seriously pray! I prayed when I had mindless work to do, I prayed through my lunch hour, and I prayed on my way home. Every night on the way home I would do some serious debriefing with the Lord. I didn't want to carry any residue of the battle into my evenings. Things just got more and more difficult. It made me want to quit, but I knew that the hand of the Lord had brought me in and that I could trust Him to carry me through. I said to Him, "Lord, I will endure this place until you think I've learned my lesson, and then please, please move me out of here."

It was so difficult! I can still remember one particular night leaving work and walking out to my car. As I approached my car, I could see the word *Die* scratched into the paint! My first thought was that it was God's message to me. Although I reported it to the police, still I knew that God was ministering to my heart through it all. I'd had a really rough day and wanted to blame it all on my coworkers. I had refused to call my feelings what they were: sin. I had chosen the way of flesh, and like many times before, I was totally busted! Yes, Lord, I hear you loud and clear. I must die to my anger, hurt, and resentment and allow you to take over.

As I got into the car, God's tender forgiveness came to my repentant heart—cleansing, release, and freedom flowed over me. I wish I could say that the rest of my days there at work were easy after that, but I can say that I learned to war and persevere and rest in God. In the end I was laid off. When that day came I was given a new job as the office manager for our growing church. And as I look back on that time, I am thankful and often remember what Paul wrote in Romans 5:3–4:

> Even in times of trouble we have a joyful confidence, knowing that our pressures will develop in us patient endurance. And patient endurance will refine our character, and proven character leads us back to hope. And this hope is not a disappointing fantasy, because we can now experience the endless love of God cascading into our hearts through the Holy Spirit who lives in us!

Just remember that Jesus walked through a desert wilderness before you did, and He will never forsake the one who follows Him across the sand. He remained faithful in His tests because He knew you would one day be His friend and follow Him wherever He leads you. Remember too that Satan was defeated in His wilderness because Jesus put His faith in the Father. And so your victory will come in the same way, by a confident trust in God no matter what comes into your life.

GOD'S WHISPER

I have a deep and tender love for you, a covenant of love between us. Expect to see My love demonstrated for you today. I have never left you on your own, even when you did not perceive My love. I have never withheld from you one thing that is the best. My love is beyond logic and discovery by the mind. It is real, even as a blanket upon you on a cold night is real. The love covenant we have together can never be broken. My love will not fail you or be diminished, even when you disappoint yourself. The strength of My love is stronger than any bond, and it burns brighter than a million suns.

I am your Fierce Protector. Who can harm you when you are locked into My heart? I love it when you trust Me and when you lean into My heart of love. I am overjoyed when you believe in My love and expect Me to work out every difficulty you face. Your trust strengthens the love covenant between us. So delight in Me, even as I delight in you. Rest in this love, for it will never fail you.

CHAPTER 16

❖

THE WILDERNESS: WHERE YOUR FRIEND IS WAITING

We will never forget a time while we were in our missionary training with New Tribes Mission that we had reached the end of our resources. We were without funds, we had only one can of bean soup in our pantry to feed our family of five, and it was dinnertime. Hunger indeed makes you desperate in prayer. We were in the phase of our training known as "boot camp," learning the lessons of God's faithfulness. (We always thought it was named that because we needed "the boot" right where it would help us the most!)

So as a family, we all knelt down on the floor of our one-room apartment and prayed. We really prayed! Hunger will drive you to that time of effectual, fervent prayer. Our oldest daughter, Charity, prayed that God would give us three things: cookies, crackers, and cereal. And within thirty minutes of praying that prayer, we heard a knock on our door. Startled, we discovered it was our friends who lived in another state. They had unexpectedly come to visit us. And in their arms were two bags of groceries!

Among other things, they gave us cookies, crackers, and cereal, even the brand of cereal Charity had asked for! On their way to visit us, our friends told us they felt the Lord had told them to stop and buy us some groceries. There is a place where promises come true. Yes, out of those wilderness circumstances, favor and refreshing will spring up.

FINDING A FRIEND IN THE DESERT

> In the desolate wilderness [God] found [Jacob]—in a barren land and an empty wasteland. There he shielded him and cared for him; he watched over him in love as the apple of his eye. And in the same way an eagle that stirs up its nest and hovers over its young, then spreads its wings to catch them and lifts them up on its pinions— so the Lord cared for them! (Deuteronomy 32:11–12)

From this passage, we learn seven major wilderness lessons. You will excel in life when you master these seven truths:

1. *Your true friend, the Living God, will watch over you to protect you from harm.*

What looks like pain is really a birthing! Something is coming forth from deep inside of you … it's Christ in you, your hope of glory. Nothing will harm you in the wilderness. It's meant to grow you into His image.

2. *He will lovingly care for you through every difficulty.*

This is where you will discover His loving-kindness. All that you truly need will be provided for you in the desert just like it is in the garden of His love. He will make your desert bloom like a rose.

3. *He will watch over you, for you are the apple of His eye.*

Even when you are in the midst of difficulty, in a barren desert, you are still His delight. He will not abandon you there. Your troubles never trouble His love for you. He has invested too much in your journey to leave you before it's finished. Love moves Him to spare nothing in guarding you night and day.

4. *He will not hesitate to stretch you and make you fly.*

In the desert, the nest is no longer comfortable. We know we must change and jump into something new. Sometimes it takes a spiritual desert to cause you to advance to higher levels. If you jump, He will catch you! You've been waiting for God to move, but He's waiting for you to move. As you move toward the direction He's leading, He will break through for you, He will open the door, and He will make a way for you. God is always far ahead on your path of impossibility. He has gone before you and is simply asking you to follow Him.

That door isn't going to open until you start walking toward it. Get moving toward your miracle!

5. *The Lord alone will be your tour guide.*

You may not realize it, but He's the One who's led you into the wilderness, and He'll be the One to lead you out of it. His covering wings of grace will be over you as the Most High keeps watch over your journey. Your desert days will bring the best out of you—Jesus Christ. You will come up out of your wilderness, leaning on your Beloved.

(6.) *The wilderness shows us the promises of God are real!*

Let's admit it. We are not really convinced of God's promises. We know He never fails, but we always seem to make an exception out of the problem we're facing. God's promises aren't real to us until we've tested them and found them to be flawless. There are times the Lord will lead us into a wilderness simply to show us He is faithful and He can be fully trusted! We quickly forget that when God promises us something, it attracts a trial—a test to prove the word God gives us. The promise is true, but it will be proven by the test attracted to the promise. This is not to torment or punish us but to prove the quality of the word we receive. God's promises are not hopeful wishes; they're powerful truths that are demonstrated by the test we are taken through when that promise comes.

(7.) *Satan will always mock us and do his best to defeat us in our wilderness—but this is where our miracle is found.*

Wilderness warfare is often intense. Every battle, every skirmish is meant to teach us how to lean into the strength of Christ, our Beloved. It's in these difficult seasons that our enemy pulls out his most devastating weapons. He'll whisper to us that it's futile to love God. He'll do his best to convince us we're missing God's plan and God has abandoned us. He'll attempt to weaken our resolve and hinder our advance as we reach further into God. It's like coming under the fog of fatigue that can cause us to lose our way.

In the desert there are mirages. Mirages are sights that are not real, such as water where there is none. A mirage of the enemy comes in the desert to deceive and pull us off God's path of personal destiny. Our focus is broken and our eyes are then turned from God's original purpose to be consumed with distractions, things that really don't matter.

While in the wilderness, it seems as if others let us down and disappoint us. The enemy will try to magnify the weaknesses of others in an attempt to offend and bring bitterness into our hearts. Yet if we are consistently turning our hearts to God, He'll protect us and heal any wounding caused by others. We can find the miracle of new strength in our difficulty as hope ignites our hearts with renewed faith.

Don't forget these seven lessons—they'll help prepare you for the glory that lies ahead!

LIVING STREAMS

We mistakenly believe that every trouble in our life is sent by Satan as the enemy of our existence. But what if we began to see our problems as a catalyst for God's restoration and miracle power? What if our wilderness is actually the canvas upon which God paints a miracle?

> I will make streams flow down from the barren heights, and springs in the middles of the valleys. I will turn the desert into pools of refreshing water, and the parched ground into flowing springs. (Isaiah 41:18)

We are convinced that God will use our circumstances to prepare us for his demonstration of miracles. You are not "up against a wall," but you are simply being groomed for the greatness of His miracle power. God will use our trouble, not to harm us but to promote us! Our impossibility pushes us into God's promises of power. Our critics become tools to make us more like Christ. The Bible describes this by using the term *refining fire*. In the Old Testament this process is also likened to a purifying fire:

> If you burn away the impurities from silver, a sterling vessel will emerge from the fire. And if you purge corruption

from the kingdom, a king's reign will be established in righteousness. (Proverbs 25:4–5)

I'm fully convinced that the One who began this glorious expression of grace in you will faithfully continue the process of maturing you through your union with him and will complete it at the unveiling of our Lord Jesus. (Philippians 1:6)

We believe every trouble in your life right now is a prophecy of the next place the door of hope will swing open for you. Be ready for new doors in the desert to take you to a place of hope and expectation!

GOD'S WHISPER

My words will mean more to you than the words that come from others. It is in My words that you find life and strength. When you are praised or when you are criticized, come back to Me and lay those words before Me. Only in My presence will you know truth. If I correct you, it is to transform you. And when I encourage you and display My love to you, receive it and rejoice in it, for it is your strength. Those places in you that have yet to be perfected will only be changed when you commune with Me in sacred intimacy. People will correct you when you are wrong, but I will heal you when you fall. My words have the power to eliminate your fears. They have grace to erase your flaws.

Listen to My words and cherish all that I say to you. When your heart condemns you, know that condemnation doesn't come from Me. I never condemn you; I am always greater than your heart. Do not seek the respect of others and thereby forget My words. Soon you will see what I visualized you to be when I gave birth to you.

Come close to Me and I will come closer to you, until you see My glory and My beauty. I have walked close with you through your childhood years, even when you did not recognize Me. And now My words are sweeter as you grow older and more tender. I am your life source, and today I am the living Word within you.

CHAPTER 17

⟡

THE WILDERNESS: A PLACE OF BEAUTY

The glories of Christ are most often hidden from us until we're ready to see them. The beautiful Jesus longs to be seen and known by hearts that have been prepared. God has a great plan for your life, and to prove it, He invested sacred blood to wash you clean and make you like Christ. Knowing this will keep you from fainting along the way. There is more to life in Christ than the myth of unbroken victory. Every mature one knows that it takes a wilderness for God to unfold His robe of beauty and show us His arm of power. When you're in a wilderness, there's no better place for your eyes to begin to focus on Him.

Have you walked through a spiritual wilderness lately? You are not alone! Not every wilderness trek is because of rebellion or sin. Jesus had no sin, yet He was led by the Spirit into the wilderness for forty days (Luke 4:1). God has a wilderness for everyone who would follow in the steps of Jesus.

We have learned in our journey together that it's in the desert-like place that God reveals Himself. He sets us apart in the desperate and desolate place. Our hearts begin to blossom as Christ emerges from within. It's then that we begin to realize the beauty that can come out of a desert place. Jesus makes any place look beautiful!

Every wilderness has a name. There was one special wilderness God brought His people into. It was the chosen place where he would uncover His beauty to His people. It was a three-day journey from Mount Sinai (where the Ten Commandments were given) to a desolate place called the wilderness of *Paran*—a Hebrew word for "beauty."

After leaving Sinai, the Israelites traveled until the glory cloud settled down and rested over them in the Desert of Paran (Numbers 10:12). The cloud led them to a desert place where God revealed Himself to their hearts. For when we ask to see His beauty and His glory, we may be asking for a wilderness where we see nothing but Him and Him alone.

It was in this wilderness of beauty that David found himself after his prophetic mentor, Samuel, passed into his reward. Even in David's grief, he witnessed the beauty of God as he found a hiding place from the persecution of Saul. This hiding place of His beauty is the true source of comfort and consolation. Bitterness mars the soul, but seeing the beauty in our pain marks the soul as one set apart for kingly favor.

MOSES AND MOUNT PARAN

Paran is where Moses gave his final blessing before he died. Listen to how he describes the wilderness of beauty:

The Lord Yahweh came to us at Sinai and rose like the dawn upon us at Seir; he appeared shining forth from

Mount Paran. He came with myriads of holy ones, his host, from his mountain slopes. Surely, he is the Lover of his people. (Deuteronomy 33:2–3)

As Israel sat waiting for God at Mount Sinai, they saw Him come in glory from the north, like a small distant storm cloud that got closer and bigger until God hovered over Sinai and the "fireworks began." This light of dawn continued to shine over them as they walked into a desert. We would love to have this glory visible over us again, wouldn't we? Yet we believe the coming sunrise of glory is meant to carry us through a day of difficulty. Glory and beauty is ahead for you, even if it is thunderbolts for the world. There is something about a wilderness walk that will glorify your soul. As you remain faithful in the test, in the days of uncertainty, the very glory and beauty of Christ emerges from within your spiritual DNA.

A BEAUTIFUL BREAKTHROUGH

I (Brian) remember days of intense pressure while in the jungle. No one seemed to listen to us as we longed to share the message of Christ with the tribal people. Their drunken fiestas dulled their hearts to the reality of Christ. We would pray for open doors, yet every heart seemed closed.

More and more I began to see that the one heart that God wanted to break open was my own. As I prayed one morning by the light of our flickering kerosene lamp, I heard the Lord whisper, *I brought you here to reach you, Brian. Until I reach into the deepest places of your heart and touch you with My glory, you'll not reach the native people with the gospel of grace. I brought you here to break you open. If I can break you open, then I can reach them.*

It was in that season of my life that I began to actually feel the presence of the beautiful God working in my ugliness, forming Christ within me. The Jesus who could convert and conform me into His image would have no problem reaching the darkest heart of those around me. A personal trek into truth began that morning as I prayed and surrendered my heart to the Lord once again, saying, "Break me open, Lord, and make me holy!"

We've found that God doesn't change our circumstances as quickly as we want Him to. Our prayers often wait for our hearts to grow into them. When we lived in the jungle, my complaints were many. It was hot, the people were hard, my days were long and difficult, and my language learning seemed to go so slow. I was tired of eating bananas and rice. But as my heart changed, my prayers were answered. God didn't deliver me from my complaints, but He took my complaints from my heart and gave me praise and beauty instead.

After my self-life was surrendered to God and burned in the fire of testing, only ashes could be found. Out of those ashes the beautiful Christ began to be formed in me and released from me. The wilderness of beauty was where Christ came forth from my ashes. Even the bananas started tasting better!

SELF-PITY

Self-pity is such a poor substitute for sacrificing our life to God! We've learned that self-pity is the devil's babysitter. It becomes a wall of defense around our soul that keeps God out and hinders us from going into the next place He has prepared for us. God's will does not spare us, pamper us, or keep us from difficult situations. God will give us all we need, but self-pity keeps us from that glorious provision that's waiting on the other side of our difficulty.

The wilderness is a place of the beautiful presence of God. He dwells there, leads us there, and reveals Himself to us there! Most of us are aware of the importance of the ark of the covenant, but have we forgotten that the entire forty years the Israelites traveled through the wilderness they took His presence with them? They carried it before them according to God's instructions. Each time they stopped, they built the tabernacle again to house it before they even set up their own tents. How about you and me? What do we do first? Sometimes we get so busy with our stuff that we don't take time to honor His presence.

God's presence was with Israel every step of the way. He didn't leave them to face the wilderness challenges alone. Perhaps you're trying to cycle out of a wilderness journey. Maybe it's time to get really serious about seeking God's presence more. As a couple, we've been personally challenged to seek and experience His manifest presence more and more—especially when we're walking through a wilderness journey. I think we'd all rather opt out of the tests that go with the journey if we could. One way we can cycle out is to determine that we'll be a witness to His manifest presence.

Many fail to realize that the ark (the presence of God) had its own wilderness journey before its arrival at Zion. The ark not only experienced a wilderness but also captivity! The enemy wants the will of God hindered in our lives. Yes, Satan would love for God's plans to bow down and submit to his demonic hindrances. Satan would also love to cause us to bow down to idolatry. For idolatry is more than bowing down to a "graven" image—it's bowing down to any false image, any untrue belief we have concerning God. An example of this would be for us to believe that God will not protect us or provide for us.

We've learned not to trust in our faith but in the Faithful One. Many times we ask God to help us when He's been helping us all along. Elisha had to encourage his servant, and he prayed that his servant's eyes would be opened to see that there were more with him than against him. And it's the same for us. There are more angels for us than against us. There's not a shortage of help, but a shortage of leaning on God, the Faithful One!

THE BEAUTY OF HUMILITY

Our pride tells us we are sufficient, we can get through it, we can weather any storm—until life crumbles around us, we keep telling ourselves that we have what it takes. God will humble us in our desert days.

Deuteronomy 8:2–3 makes the purpose very clear:

> And you must never forget how the Lord your God brought you these forty years through the wilderness, leading you each step. He did this to humble you and test you, to discover what was in your heart, and see if you would keep his commandments or not. So he humbled you, allowed you to hunger, and then he fed you with mystery-manna which you and your ancestors had never seen before, so that he might make you realize that man must not live by bread alone; but by every word that proceeds from the mouth of the Lord.

Notice the reason why God brought them through the wilderness: it was to humble their hearts before Him. The Hebrew word used here for "humble" is *anah*, which is translated a number of ways. It can mean "humble, meek, poor, weak, afflicted," but it is also used in certain contexts to signify a response, such as, "to answer, respond, testify, speak, shout, and sing." And there is yet another meaning to *anah*, which is, "to be occupied, busied with something." The semantic range of meaning for this

Hebrew term suggests that God does use affliction and hardship to humble us but never to humiliate us. He uses the wilderness as a tool to cause us to be occupied or busied with Him and Him alone until we break out on the other side singing and shouting his praises! God doesn't leave us in a humble, low place, for He delights to raise up the humble and lift them up on high! Haven't you found this to be true?

A Crown of Beauty

In the place of devastation, God can bring a crown of beauty; ashes are replaced with beauty (Isaiah 61:3). God has shown up for us time after time. After Satan may throw his worst at you, God will bestow His best upon you—a crown of beauty! We don't just survive; we can thrive in a wilderness. Hidden in your surroundings today are secret surprises, beauty waiting to emerge. As you remain faithful, never giving into fear or despair, your ashes will be changed into beauty. A shining, glistening crown of beauty will be placed on your brow, and it will be seen by those around you. Just wait. You'll see.

GOD'S WHISPER

My words are meant for you! My words mean more than any words spoken by anyone in your life. Let My words overwhelm you and heal you from the wounds of your journey. Come and listen to the Words that come from My mouth. They are words of healing and words of grace. For it is in My words that you will find life and strength. If I correct you, it is to transform you. Don't be disappointed in what I speak to you. Receive deeply into your innermost being, and it will be power and authority within you. The matters of your heart that have distracted your focus can only be removed as you become intimate with Me. My words have power to eliminate your fears and soothe your soul. You will listen to My words that I speak this day and cherish all that I say. Remember, when your heart condemns you, I will not. I will erase your flaws, for I am greater than your heart and know all things. Rest in the shelter of My faithfulness.

CHAPTER 18

✤

THE WILDERNESS:
WHERE HE ALLURES US

Just pause for a moment, think about your life, and consider the surprises that are awaiting you in your wilderness. They're not disappointing surprises but pleasant ones. For God transforms His people in the wilderness, not in a school, a clinic, or in a worship service. It takes a wilderness to teach us how to lean upon our Beloved. Miracles are waiting to manifest in each and every wilderness.

Most of the miracles we read about in the Bible were worked in a wilderness. Joshua wasn't in a church service when he spoke to the sun and it stood still. He was way out in a wilderness of fighting foes and winning wars. God's desire is to teach us the way of victory in these times as we let Him have His way. Instead, too many of us let ourselves be thrown into depression or discouragement when we are led into a wilderness season. Promises seem like they will never be fulfilled, God seems distant, emotions seem flat, and our strength fades. These are times when

God is weaning us from our self-life and showing us how truly inadequate we are.

The wilderness is where we experience the "de-selfing" of our lives. And every spiritual discovery is good, even the ones that point to our weaknesses. In fact, we are told to rejoice in trials:

> May the thought of this cause you to jump for joy, even though lately you've had to put up with the grief of so many trials, but these only reveal the sterling core of your faith, which is far more valuable than gold which perishes, for even gold is refined by fire. And your undying faith will result in even more praise, glory, and honor when Jesus the Anointed One is revealed! You love him passionately although you did not see him, but through believing in him you are saturated with an ecstatic joy, indescribably sublime and immersed in glory! For you are reaping the harvest of your faith—the full salvation promised you—your souls' victory! (1 Peter 1:6–9)

The Lord knows how deeply we love Him, and He knows that love must be made perfect and mature. Our difficult seasons of life "season" us and shape our love as one who is abandoned to God, no matter what. You must make room in your understanding of God for His furious love. It's so furious that it holds nothing back that will make you more like Christ.

Where do we discover the true dimensions of the love of God? Where do we learn its depth and height? We find the furious love of the Bridegroom when He takes us into the desert experience. It's the place where we give up the myth of trying to please God in our self-life, our flesh. We must be broken in the wilderness so we can blossom like a rose.

In a wilderness setting, our secondary loves are revealed and exposed before our eyes. We love our comforts and our conveniences, but most of all, we love our control of things. So much of our lives are spent in making sure we get what we want. In the wilderness, God gets what He wants—more of our hearts.

There we're stripped of false affections and other masters besides Him. In this place of divine encounter, His voice is heard and His heart is revealed. Jesus becomes the one and only love of our life.

Let's read from the ancient writings of the prophet Hosea:

> "I am now going to allure [God's people] with open arms, I will lead her into the desert [wilderness] and there I will speak tenderly to her. There I will give her back her vineyards, and I will transform the Valley of Trouble into an open door of hope. She will sing there, responding to me as she did in the days of her youth … and in that day," declares the Lord, "you will call me, 'my Husband'; you will no longer call me, 'my Master' … and I will take you to be my wife forever!" (Hosea 2:14–16, 19)

That doesn't sound too bad to me.

Our time with Jesus can be the most thrilling time of our day. It's in that holy place that we encounter our majestic Bridegroom. Never will you experience anything more enthralling than what you taste and see in the courts of His presence. Yet this Bridegroom has some funny ways of leading us … leading us where we would never choose to go. Like into a desert: "I am now going to allure her with open arms" (v. 14).

Can you get the picture of God "alluring" you, even tricking you to go into a place you would not choose if it were up to you? What does this mean? The Hebrew word used here for *allure* can also be translated "to flatter, to persuade, to enlarge"—one Bible teacher suggested that it could even be translated "to be silly." Sounds like God is lovingly being playful with us! He stands at the threshold of our heart and says, *Come on out into the wilderness, let's play! I want to share my secrets with you!*

The wilderness is a place of surprises, a land of hide-and-seek. It's the place where we discover miracles even in our need. Your Beloved Friend loves you so much that He's willing to stake His reputation on your spiritual growth. He wants to rejoice over you with singing and laughter. He spins you around in the wilderness until you can do nothing but be carried in His arms—and He loves it that way! Really, the desert doesn't sound that bad, for if the wilderness shows me the love of God, then maybe I need the wilderness.

Let us speak from our experience. It seems at times that God tricked us into going with Him to places we never asked for. Some of the difficulties we experienced as a family in the jungle we don't remember asking for: our daughter bitten by a Bushmaster snake, the loss of all our possessions in a flooding river, sicknesses, or the threats of death.

We remember praying together so many times, "Lord, use us!" And because of His deep love for us, this is how He interpreted our prayer: *Lord, go ahead and break us so completely that we are beyond repair, ruined, and devastated. Let people walk all over us if that's what You want, but use us, Lord!*

God interprets our prayers quite differently than the way we verbalize them. How many times have you found the Lord leading you into a situation where you ended up humiliated, even broken? But actually this is what we are asking for when we say, "Lord, I want You! Do whatever it takes for me to have more room in my life for You!"

When we pray, "Show me Your glory, show me Your face!" He takes us, like He did Moses and the Israelites, into the wilderness to show us. Don't be surprised by the way God chooses to answer your prayers. The Father really does know best.

THE TENDERNESS OF GOD

God says in Hosea 2:14, "I will lead her into the desert and *speak tenderly* to her" (emphasis added). There is a loving voice we will hear in the desert, the place of tender speaking. When we are weary, wanting to give up, and discouraged over our lack of progress in the ways of God, that's when He comes. He comes us with tender remedy. He comes with His acceptance, His unfailing love, and His tender embrace. And His kindness overwhelms our fear as we call out to God in our wilderness.

Here are some lovely Scriptures from the book of Isaiah. They've been our strength in a weary land. Read them slowly, carefully. Really take a look at these verses and think about the kindness of God and His tender ways when you have been the most disappointed:

Even the desert will bloom like a rose. Every dry and barren place will blossom abundantly, singing joyously of the new day! (Isaiah 35:1–2)

"Have compassion on my people! Oh tenderly comfort them," says your God. "Speak softly and tenderly to Jerusalem, but also make it very clear that she has served her sentence, that her sin is taken care of—forgiven! She's been punished enough and more than enough, and now it's over and done with." (40:1–2)

Like a shepherd, he will care for his flock, gathering the lambs in his arms, hugging them as he carries them. (40:11)

God will lead his blind people along an unknown path, one never seen before. He will make their dark mystery bright with light, and smooth their difficult road. He will straighten every crooked thing in front of them so they can move forward without fear, they will never be forsaken. (42:16)

"Look! I'm about to do something I've never done before! It will spring up right in front of your eyes—can't you recognize what I'm doing? I will open up streams in the desert and paths through the wilderness." (43:19)

In your most difficult moment—when life isn't working for you—the tender voice of the Bridegroom will be heard. He never forsakes the one whose heart is reaching for Him.

At times, we need more than just a tender voice; we need a miracle! We need restoration and provision to make it through the wilderness seasons of our lives. Hosea says it this way: "There I will give her back her vineyards" (2:15).

In the desert, we can have our "vineyard" restored. The vineyard speaks of abundance, new wine, overflowing joy, and supernatural life. Restoration can be found in the dry desert. Miracles won't always be seen on the mountaintops in front of everybody so they can applaud us. Miracles will be seen in the wilderness where God alone will receive the glory. No one will be able to say it was our hands or our "anointing" that made it happen.

God, glorify your name!
Yes, your name alone be glorified, not ours!
For you are the One who loves us passionately,
and you are faithful and true. (Psalm 115:1)

At times, the Holy Spirit will allow deep pain to resurface in a wilderness season. We thought it was gone forever, but there it rises within us again. Why? So that full and complete restoration may be experienced. God delights in true maturity coming forth in our vineyard. Not just shriveled grapes, but full, ripe, mature vines loaded with the joy of the Lord. A desert develops us into the image of Christ. Just as John the Baptist introduced Jesus to the people in the wilderness, the Holy Spirit shows us who Jesus really is in our desert wandering.

A Door of Hope

God's ways are funny and at times seemingly strange as we consider how He deals with us and shows us His heart. Listen to this and come with me to the place where troubles turn into triumph!

"I will make the Valley of Trouble into an open door of hope." (Hosea 2:15)

No matter what trouble you've had to walk through this week, God promises to make it into a gateway of glory. God is so full of power that He can transform every trial into a supernatural opportunity—a door of hope in the wilderness.

Everyone passes through trouble—no one is exempt, no one gets a hall pass or a detour around difficulty. Yet inside of the believer there is a big difference. We may pass through similar matters of pain and affliction, but we have an open door to a revelation of hope. What a difference! God will not only bring us through, but He will also open a door of hope and triumph.

Sooner or later you'll find yourself in the Valley of Trouble, a common denominator for every child of God. And when we find ourselves there, we must remember to hold onto hope and abandon despair. For it's in the Valley of Trouble that we may actually be brought into a new, exhilarating relationship with God, a relationship so rich in meaning that it's like a marriage. "In that day," we will call Him "my Husband" (Hosea 2:16). Sounds like romance waiting in our misfortune.

The Hebrew word for "trouble" is *achor*. It was in the Valley of Achor that Achan sinned and brought grief and devastation to the people of God (Joshua 7). This is when he was found out, sentenced to die, stoned, and left buried under the rocks that were thrown at him. Have you ever had the shame of guilt try to bury you? God wants to take all your shame, brokenness, and disgrace and turn it into an opportunity for advancement, ministry, and breakthrough. God wants to make our Valley of Achor a door of hope.

Achor represented the trouble and pain one person's sin can bring upon many others. In time, the Valley of Achor came to symbolize the worst of punishments. It was a place of death and desolation. Today, of course, we don't stone those whose sin or irresponsibility has caused others grief. Still, sin has consequences, and though we may not be physically stoned for our failure, the effects of public condemnation can be just as crushing to the human spirit. The fact is that too many of us have known a personal Valley of Achor where our moral negligence or ill-advised actions have caused another's suffering.

Always remember that our Redeemer came to proclaim liberty to those who are "prisoners" (see Isaiah 61:1), those held captive by their deeds. He came on behalf of all of us who are prisoners of our past failures. Jesus came to deliver and restore those whose dreams lie buried in the Valley of Achor.

It's true. God will allure us into the wilderness, but only to show us how faithful, how beautiful, and how gracious He is to us. What lessons the wilderness can teach us! If you feel like you are being "allured" into a new experience, even into what seems daunting and unpredictable, don't lose heart. You are more than His servant; you are His spouse, His beloved, His chosen one. Trust in His love, and you will see Him as a faithful Bridegroom, the Beloved of your soul.

GOD'S WHISPER

The fruitfulness of My blessing will increase in your life from this day onward. My blessings will multiply even as your sorrows shrink and fade away. Although you have seen trouble, now you will see hope and blessing rise upon you. The place of your deepest wound is a prophecy of where I will heal you. In that failure I have given you a gift—the wide-open door of hope! Come inside that doorway, and you will discover what every longing soul has found—satisfaction in Me. I will not relent until I have restored to you the joy of your youth, the song of your first love devotion to Me. You will sing again. Your song will awaken the hearts of sleeping ones. Your voice is sweet to Me, and your face is lovely. You will see My hand of love shape your life like never before. Your days of living in a valley of discouragement are over. Today you will rise and come away with Me. I am Your Bridegroom, not merely your Master. Arise, My love, and come away!

✤

CHAPTER 19

THE WILDERNESS: WHERE WE LEARN TO LEAN ON OUR BELOVED

God alone has the power to turn our troubles into triumph. Through the prophet Hosea, God promises His people, "I will transform the Valley of Trouble into an open door of hope!" (2:15). Every mistake of our past is but the prelude of a miracle waiting to be seen and heard. Failure is the back door to success. Messes become miracles as we turn our hearts from the past to walk through the inviting, open door of hope.

God loves us so much that He may design a unique holding pattern for our lives until we grow more like Christ. And the wilderness is His waiting room. It's in this waiting room that we learn patience until we can rise up like an eagle. If you've ever felt as if God were holding you back, just know that He's done it out of love for you. He doesn't want to see all that He's already done in you crumble. His desire is that you reach your destiny fully prepared. He loves you that much!

When we seem delayed in our journey by the wilderness experience, Jesus comes as a Bridegroom and says: "Place me as a seal over your heart!" (Song of Songs 8:6). What a promise, that Jesus would "seal" us in His love with acceptance and tender mercy. Did you know that the Hebrew word for "seal" in Song of Songs 8:6 is actually the Hebrew word for "prison cell"? Jesus comes with such strong love that it imprisons us with hope. The seal over our heart is a prison cell of holy love—that makes us all prisoners of the Lord!

Your fortress in this season is trusting in a loving God. He's your refuge. How can you run from your true refuge? So, return, beloved, to your fortress and remain a prisoner of hope until He decides you're ready for all that He has for you. What now feels like a prison cell to you, God sees as a fortress. It's a great place to hide until the Valley of Trouble becomes a door of hope!

YOU WILL SING AGAIN

Isn't it thrilling when our heart overflows in His presence and we lift up songs to delight His heart? Yet the most pure, powerful, and intimate song of worship will come in the wilderness!

> "I am now going to allure her [God's people]; I will lead her into the wilderness and speak tenderly to her. There I will give her back her vineyards, and will make the Valley of Achor [Trouble] a door of hope. There she will respond as in the day she came out of Egypt. "In that day," declares the LORD, "you will call me 'my husband'; you will no longer call me 'my master.' … I will betroth you to me [take you to be my wife] forever …" (Hosea 2:14–16, 19 NIV)

Such comfort and joy can come in the wilderness. All the past trouble will be a doorway to a new beginning. All of the lessons we learn will be turned back on the devil. Where we once complained, we will sing. This is the paradox of the wilderness!

Many times we ask, *Why, Lord? Why do I have to go through this?* He is saying two words: *Worship Me.* The Bible says, "Worship in awe and wonder, all you who've been made holy! For all who fear him will feast with plenty" (Psalm 34:9).

When we're facing our darkest hour, we need to focus on God the most. It's in the crisis, the chaos, the confusion, and the times when we feel out of control that we really need to focus on Him. When your heart is breaking, the healing God simply says, "Worship Me!"

Nothing is more pleasing to God than a human heart surrounded by disappointment that still worships Him. Worship is more real and authentic when it is in the midst of painful situations. We have a theory that when we get to heaven and the Lord shows us the things He loved most about our journey, He will show us those times when we worshiped Him during a dark season of our soul. The incense of praise turns sweeter when the days around us are darker.

We were so burdened at times in our jungle experience that we wanted to escape, run away, and hide like frightened children. But God knew we had nowhere to run! We were surrounded by a tropical rainforest with no roads and no cruise ship to take us away. But our burdens lifted when we sang. There were numerous times our precious Paya-Kuna friends would come into our hut and overhear us singing and simply loving on Jesus. In our distress, with no cell phones available to call an encouraging friend, we found that all we could do was worship. The song of the Lord took away the pain of self-focus! Our native friends would sit and listen to us sing in English, not understanding what we were saying, but sensing the sweet presence of God as we worshiped.

WHERE WE FIND THE BRIDEGROOM

It takes a wilderness to be weaned from self-love and to be prepared for the passion of the Bridegroom. The revelation of the Bridegroom God is waiting for us in the land of "I wish I weren't here"!

To know God as our loving Master is good. But to know Him as our Beloved Bridegroom is better. One is a relationship of boss/servant. The other is a relationship of love/union. In the wilderness, our works dry up and shrivel. We have no boast, and there's nothing in our flesh that can rescue us. We all go in as a servant, but we come up and out as the bride—with loyal love that leans upon the Bridegroom's chest.

The wilderness forces us to be intimate with Jesus. It's in the wilderness that our Bridegroom transforms us into the bride, for our difficulties were designed to bring us into His heart. In the desert our garden becomes His garden, and He takes possession of our soul.

Here's a question to ponder: Have your trials become heavier than your theology? It's amazing how our difficulties bring out our doubts. What we really believe is what we really believe when we're facing the most difficult season in life: the wilderness days. But when we see the King as our Bridegroom, the one who allured us into that wilderness with a forever love, we melt, give up the struggle, and abandon our soul to Him.

If you will remain faithful in the "stretchings" of faith and through the conflict, then you will eventually hear the breaking in of His voice of affection. The Hebrew word translated as "desert" in Hosea 2:14 literally means "the place of speaking." All that

Jesus has waited so long to teach us, He will reveal in the wilderness. His miracles of love are the best miracles of all!

Imagine all the things that you have had to go through in your life up to this point. These are the things that He uses to escort you to the heart of your eternal husband, your partner forever! Every test is an invitation to trust Him more fully. Soon, and very soon, all the difficulties of the past will be forgotten and the light of Christ's presence will make our darkness turn to day.

He has a reason for alluring us into the wilderness, for He desires to bring us to a discovery that makes it all worth it! Look beyond the momentary mess and see the eternal ecstasy that waits just around the bend. Can you continue on until you see your Bridegroom, your Beloved King, face-to-face?

GOD'S WHISPER

Today you stand at the threshold of a new beginning. All that is around you will change, and all that I have planted within you will now grow and bear fruit. For I have great things in store for you, things no one has ever proclaimed to you. Many speak of the rain that will soon fall, but I say, it will be a downpour on you! Many speak of the fire, but they have never been consumed. But with you, My fire will rage and not be contained by the structures and theories of men. There are many who wish for a new day, but you will be lifted suddenly into a season beyond your imagination or your dreams. For it will be My dream that will be fulfilled in your life. So stand firm in Me until I have become your confidence. Set your eyes upon Me and don't be worried about your future and your calling, for I am the God who begins and completes, the Alpha and the Omega. You have seen Me many times as the Beginning, now you will see Me as the Finisher!

CHAPTER 20

THE WILDERNESS:
WHERE WE FIND HOPE

So many in the body of Christ are in the wilderness and wondering if they're going to make it through. If that's you today, I have good news for you. First of all, you're not alone. We all experience it, because we're all led through this way of the wilderness. Secondly, God wants us to cross over out of our wilderness into the land flowing with milk and honey, a realm full of glory and fulfilled promises. Beloved, He did not lead you to the wilderness so that you would die there:

> I pray with great faith for you, because I'm fully convinced that the One who began this glorious work of grace in you will faithfully continue the process of maturing you and will complete it at the unveiling of our Lord Jesus Christ! (Philippians 1:6)

Are you chained to hopelessness, or are you anchored to hope? Our hope is not wishful fantasy, based on something in us or even around us. Our hope is an anchor that has gone inside the veil in glory. Our hope is Christ, who is the anchor of our soul both sure and steadfast.

There is hope for everyone in your family to be born again and filled with the Spirit, loving God and loving each other. There is hope for your city, your church, your marriage, and your finances. Hope for your body, soul, and spirit. There is hope for your future!

At times we stop and have to remind ourselves of the lessons God has taught us. It seems we forget in the dark what God revealed to us in the light. So we speak to each other and remind ourselves of a number of the hope lessons. Can we share them with you?

We remind ourselves that God is truly in control. He's the One in charge of our lives and our futures. And we are compelled to remember there is an eternal life to come. What we suffer now is nothing compared to the glory He will give us later (Romans 8:18). Remember, "He will keep you steady and strong to the very end, making you mature in character so that no one will accuse you of anything—innocent on the day of our Lord Jesus Christ" (1 Corinthians 1:8).

Don't let any voice say to you, "It's over. Your life is finished!" Time after time, the Bible records hopeless situations that ultimately ended in victory. Think of Job's sickness, Joseph's betrayal by his brothers, David's adultery, and the many who were healed in mind, body, and spirit. God has not given up on you! His plans for your life can never be thwarted:

> When it seems as though you are facing nothing but difficulties see it as an individual opportunity to experience all the joy that you can for you know that when your faith is tested it stirs up power within you to endure all things.

And then as your endurance grows even stronger it will release perfection into every part of your being until there is nothing missing and nothing lacking. (James 1:2–4)

REMEMBER—YOU ARE LOVED

Perhaps this is the most important hope lesson to remember: God does love you! He sees your suffering and weeps with you. Your prayers are heard: "Do you know of any parent who would give his hungry child, who asked for food, a plate of rocks instead? Or when asked for a piece of fish, what parent would offer his child a snake instead?" (Matthew 7:9–10).

We can promise you this: whatever you're facing, you are not facing it alone. God has said, "I will never leave you alone, never! And I will not loosen my grip on your life." So we can say with great confidence: "I know the Lord is for me and I will never be afraid of what people may do to me!" (Hebrews 13:5–6).

Beloved, the Lord is leading His bride into the wilderness. Knowing what you know now, will you follow? Will you sing and run after Him? Will you allow Him to cause you to be occupied with only Him?

GOD'S WHISPER

I have purposes for your life that began before mountains and hills were brought forth. I planned for your redemption before you saw the light of day. I opened your eyes to see the beauty of My Son, and you believed. Now My very life lives within you. I have caused you to mature, to grow in the ways of heaven as My life overtakes yours.

My grace has caused you to grow, and I am pleased; it is a good work that I have begun in you. Yet today I come with fresh wind and energy to make you even stronger. I will make Myself real to you this day, and My living presence will lift you higher. Come and grow stronger as you live in Me. My fruits will now come forth out of your innermost being. Love will prevail, and joy will absorb your pain. Peace will surround you as a cloud of glory while kindness streams from you to others. The strength of My patience will consume your anxiety. Watch as my gentleness makes you great and brings honor to your door.

I will cause My strength to overshadow you and give you courage and discipline to move ahead. I have purposes for you that embrace eternity, and I have now begun to hasten those purposes to completion. For I have chosen you before time began to live in the fullness of My Spirit. Surrender to Me this day and do not hinder My Spirit's work to make you into the image of My Son, and you will see the miracles I will perform in you.

✧

CHAPTER 21

WILDERNESS IN THE WORD

A number of wildernesses are named in the Bible. Some of them you may be familiar with. We've included this brief study to help you understand how vital it is that we grow, mature in our faith, and come up out of our wilderness leaning upon our Beloved. The name of the wilderness becomes the theme of the lesson God teaches us there.

1. *The wilderness of* **Etham**—*no turning back.*

This was the edge of the wilderness. The Hebrews had committed to move forward no matter what. This is the threshold of faith. Our faith becomes our security, not our surroundings (Exodus 13:20). Etham becomes a boundary line that is crossed, a Rubicon for those true followers of the Way who walk by faith and not by sight:

> The Lord went before them to lead them each step of the way. (Exodus 13:21)

The lesson we learn at Etham is that God will lead us forward, not backward. His advance for us means turning our backs on all that is familiar and going into the undiscovered country of walking by faith. The cloud of glory will now be our compass. We will move by his direction, not by reason or the logic of clever leaders. God will be our guide at Etham.

The word *Etham* means "solid and enduring." So is our faith, which, when tested, becomes more precious than fine gold. Faith is the solid substance we stand upon, and it is one of the three enduring virtues (1 Corinthians 13:13).

2. *The wilderness of the Red Sea—where miracles are born.*

The Red Sea is literally in Hebrew, "the Sea of Reeds." This was not simply a place of red water,* for the Hebrew word for the Sea of Reeds is *suf*. However, *suf* has a dual meaning. It can mean "reeds," but the root meaning is actually "to come to an end, to cease, to be destroyed." This is the place where all our past life comes to an end, washed in that water and removed from us forever. It wasn't only our enemies that drowned at the Red Sea. This wilderness of the Red Sea also points us to our union with Christ, which makes us one with Him in His death, burial, and resurrection. The past is gone, for we died with Christ and now can move forward with Him into a life of supernatural power and miracles. This wilderness has been designed by God that we might gain a new faith in His power and be delivered from our impossible situations.

3. *The wilderness of Shur—where everything looks impossible.*

Shur means "a wall," or "hemmed in." When you face this wilderness, you will feel like you are "up against a wall" with no place

---

* A reddish species of cyanobacteria blooms frequently in the Red Sea, giving its normally blue-green waters a reddish look at certain times.

WILDERNESS IN THE WORD

to go. It seems at that point that there is no way out. But the same God who led the Hebrews will use this wilderness to push you into your breakthrough. This was one of the first wildernesses Israel experienced, but it led them to the miracle of the Red Sea (Exodus 15:22). The wall forced them to move up against the obstacle of the Red Sea. When all hope was lost, God stepped in. This is where we learn that our limitations are but miracles in hiding.

4. *The wilderness of* Sinai—*where our hearts are exposed.*

The Hebrew word for Sinai means "thorn bush." It was God Himself who came down at Sinai and appeared to Moses first in a thorn bush. Would you be willing to go into that wilderness if it meant having a divine encounter with the God whose name is "I AM"?

Thorns in the Bible speak of the curse of sin. When Adam and Eve fell in the garden, God cursed the ground (not them!) and said that thorns and thistles would be the result of the curse of sin. When Jesus was crucified, He carried that curse for us as He wore a crown of thorns! This is a wilderness where the curse of sin is broken from us. Many glorious manifestations of God took place in this wilderness.

However, another meaning for Sinai is "miry," as in "miry clay." This is what you and I are made from. We are jars of clay. This miry substance can still carry the miracle power of God. At Sinai, sin is exposed, our "thorns" are made known to us, like a thorn in the flesh, and our miry clay is subdued by God's mighty hand.

5. *The wilderness of* Paran—*where the desert blossoms like a rose.*

This is so different than every other wilderness. It is the experience of finding beauty where others only see desolation. It is the prophetic wilderness where perfection emerges within us. The Hebrew word *Paran* means "beauty," or "glory." Most of us never see this initially as the place of beauty, but rather a place of testing. Yet every wilderness test is to bring greater beauty and glory into our lives.

It was here in Paran that the beautiful glory cloud appeared over the wilderness (Numbers 10:12). God is waiting for you to look up and see the beauty and glory He is forming in your life, even through the wilderness testing. The cloud will lead you to Paran, with its burning fire by night and shade of glory by day. We learn in Paran to stop grumbling and complaining and see the greater purpose of every difficulty.

6. *The wilderness of Sin—where sons become soldiers.*

The Hebrew word *Sin* is actually the word for "clay." This is the wilderness of clay. Here is where God molds, shapes, forms, and fashions His sons and daughters into an army of faithful soldiers. The Master Potter takes our clay in His hands and squeezes us into shape. Have you felt God's hand squeeze you lately? It is His plan to make you into a mighty warrior who will win every battle and implement His kingdom purposes on the earth.

Yet it was in this wilderness of clay that the people of Israel murmured and complained against Moses and his leadership (Exodus 16:1–3). When God squeezes us, we often become cranky, disappointed with ourselves and our environment. But this too is part of our training for reigning. We must cast off our grumbling and embrace God's perfect plan for our life, until we can walk through hard places with grace and patience. There are many battles ahead, so the hand of omnipotence must continue His work in our lives until we reflect the image of the One who holds us.

7. *The wilderness of Kedemoth—the place of steady progress.*

The word *Kedemoth* means "to advance, to make progress, to go eastward." In this desert land, the people of God had to move forward. The wilderness is not our stopping point, but something we pass through in order to reach our destiny. Lessons are learned here about not turning to the right or to the left and moving forward one step at a time.

But *Kedemoth* can also be translated "to comfort." There is comfort found in knowing that we are moving forward, not getting stuck at one place in our life. To remain in place when God says to go forward will eventually bring defeat in our lives. Israel made peace with the descendants of Esau in this wilderness (Deuteronomy 2:27–29). Our forward progress should always be marked with making peace with others in God's family. There will always be those believers who choose to antagonize, but our calling is to make peace wherever possible.

8. *The wilderness of Beersheba—the place of wandering.*

The first mention of this wilderness is in Genesis 21:14 and involves Hagar being cast out of Abraham's entourage. Hagar left camp and "wandered in the wilderness of Beersheba." She was helpless, lost, and didn't know where to go. Have you felt that way in your life? This is a wilderness you must quickly abandon for the resting place of God's love. A wandering life must come to the realization of our own inadequacies and understand that God alone is enough. This is the classroom of heaven where God teaches us His ways: that without Him we can do nothing. So the wandering brings us to the discovery of our need of God. Anything that brings you closer to God must be viewed as a blessing in the end. You will come up out of this wilderness as you lean into the loving heart and mighty strength of God. Only His resources can get us through to the place of victory.

9. *The wilderness of* Moab—*avoid it!*

We pass through some wildernesses because it is in God's merciful plan for us to hear His voice and learn from Him. But no follower of Jesus should ever pass through two wildernesses named in the Bible—the wilderness of Moab is one of them! The first mention of Moab in the Scriptures is dealing with an incestuous relationship between Lot and his oldest daughter (Genesis 19:36–37). The child born of this sin was named Moab, which means "he came from his father." Moab was destined to have no part in the inheritance of Israel (Deuteronomy 2:9), and the children of Israel were to have no part with Moab. This is the wilderness of nothing but defeat and turning away from God. It was in the field of Moab that Midian met total defeat (Genesis 36:35). This is the wilderness that belongs to those who have turned away from God's best for their lives, hardened their hearts, and refused to walk away from the sin. You will not face this wilderness, for you are an overcomer who has chosen to follow Jesus no matter what the cost.

10. *The wilderness of* Bethaven—*avoid it!*

Our final named wilderness in the Bible is the wilderness of Bethaven, which means "the house of wickedness."* This would be one place a follower of Jesus would never want to visit. It is where darkness is chosen over light, stubbornness over tenderness, and wickedness over purity.

---

* *Bethaven* is a compound word: *beth* means "house of" and *aven* means "wickedness." The word *aven* is also translated "idol" in Isaiah 66:3.

So of the ten named wildernesses, eight are places you may pass through on your way to your full inheritance in Christ. The wilderness is not to break you but to shape you. It is the place where God speaks, the place where we see his beauty, and the place where we give our all to Him. Rest assured, you will not remain in the wilderness, for you will one day leave them all behind as you rest upon the chest of your amazing High Priest and Bridegroom of your soul.

May you find comfort and strength in that place where you find yourself today. And know that God's eyes are keeping watch over you and His heart of love is marking out the path before you. We pray for you, that your eyes will open ever more fully to the wonder and beauty of your King, our Lord Jesus Christ!

Who is this one? Look at her now!

She arises out of her desert, clinging to her beloved.

When I awakened you under the apple tree,

as you were feasting upon me,

I awakened your innermost being with the travail of birth

as you longed for more of me.

Fasten me upon your heart as a seal of fire forevermore.

This living, consuming flame

will seal you as my prisoner of love.

My passion is stronger

than the chains of death and the grave,

all consuming as the very flashes of fire

from the burning heart of God.

Place this fierce, unrelenting fire over your entire being.

Rivers of pain and persecution

will never extinguish this flame.

Endless floods will be unable

to quench this raging fire that burns within you.

Everything will be consumed.

It will stop at nothing

as you yield everything to this furious fire

until it won't even seem to you like a sacrifice anymore.

—Song of Songs 8:5-7